Mediterranean Meal Prep for Beginners

150 Wholesome Recipes to Simplify Your Weekly Meals.
Your Guide to Deliciously Organized Cooking

TheoGray

TABLE OF CONTENTS

INTRODUCTION 1

CHAPTER 1 BREAKFAST AND BRUNCH RECIPES 3

    Overnight Oats with Chia, Honey, and Berries 5
    Shakshuka with Feta and Herbs 6
    Mediterranean Veggie Frittata 8
    Olive Oil and Sea Salt Avocado Toast 10
    Greek Yogurt Parfait with Granola and Pomegranate 11
    Mediterranean Breakfast Burrito 12
    Baked Oatmeal with Apples, Cinnamon, and Pecans 14
    Spinach and Feta Stuffed Portobello Mushrooms 16
    Mediterranean Breakfast Bowls with Quinoa, Eggs, and Veggies 18
    Whole Wheat Pancakes with Blueberry Compote 20
    Egg and Veggie Stuffed Pita Pockets 22
    Mediterranean Breakfast Salad with Farro, Eggs, and Olives 23
    Baked Eggs in Tomato Cups with Basil and Parmesan 25
    Tropical Chia Seed Pudding with Mango and Coconut Milk 27
    Mediterranean Breakfast Skillet with Sausage and Roasted Veggies 28
    Zucchini Fritters with Tzatziki Dipping Sauce 30
    Lentil and Egg Breakfast Bowl with Feta and Olives 32
    Mediterranean Breakfast Quiche with Spinach and Feta 33
    Baked Oatmeal Cups with Apricots and Almonds 35
    Mediterranean Breakfast Sandwiches with Roasted Red Pepper Spread 37
    Yogurt, Granola, and Fruit Parfait Jars 39
    Chickpea and Vegetable Breakfast Hash 40
    Spinach and Feta Breakfast Wraps 42
    Baked Eggs in Tomato Sauce with Olives and Feta 43
    Breakfast Quinoa Bowl with Figs, Nuts, and Honey 45

CHAPTER 2 DELICIOUS LUNCH AND DINNER IDEAS 47

    Mediterranean Chickpea and Tuna Salad 49
    Roasted Beet and Farro Salad with Goat Cheese 50
    Grilled Zucchini and Feta Salad with Lemon Herb Dressing 52
    Mediterranean Quinoa and Cucumber Salad with Dill 54
    Tomato and Mozzarella Salad with Basil Pesto 55
    Baked Mediterranean Salmon with Roasted Veggies 57

Lamb and Eggplant Moussaka 59
Mediterranean Chicken and Orzo Skillet... 61
Stuffed Portobello Mushrooms with Feta and Spinach.......................... 63
Mediterranean Vegetable and Quinoa Stuffed Peppers 65
Roasted Lemon-Garlic Potatoes with Oregano 67
Mediterranean Cauliflower Rice Pilaf 68
Baked Feta and Tomato Orzo 70
Mediterranean Roasted Vegetable Medley 72
Herbed Chickpea and Artichoke Dip with Pita Chips 74
Roasted Garlic and Lemon Broccoli 76
Mediterranean Quinoa Tabbouleh 77
Baked Feta and Spinach Stuffed Tomatoes 78
Roasted Red Pepper and Walnut Hummus with Pita Bread 79
Grilled Zucchini Rolls with Ricotta and Herbs....................................... 81
Mediterranean Bulgur Wheat Salad with Cucumber and Feta............. 82
Baked Eggplant Parmesan Stacks.. 83
Mediterranean Lentil and Sweet Potato Patties 85
Roasted Garlic and Herb Olive Oil Bread Dip 86
Mediterranean Vegetable Couscous Salad.. 88

CHAPTER 3 DELICIOUS LUNCH AND DINNER IDEAS 91

Baked Mediterranean Cod with Tomatoes and Olives........................... 93
Grilled Swordfish Kebabs with Lemon-Herb Marinade 94
Mediterranean Shrimp Scampi with Zucchini Noodles......................... 96
Baked Stuffed Calamari with Spinach and Feta 97
Mediterranean Tuna Stuffed Avocados... 99
Grilled Salmon Skewers with Mediterranean Salsa 100
Baked Mediterranean Halibut with Lemon-Caper Sauce.................... 102
Mediterranean-Style Roasted Shrimp and Vegetables 104
Mediterranean Tuna and White Bean Salad Lettuce Wraps............... 106
Baked Mediterranean Tilapia with Tomato-Olive Topping................. 107
Grilled Mediterranean Swordfish Steaks with Lemon-Herb Gremolata........ 109
Mediterranean Shrimp and Feta Stuffed Portobello Mushrooms...... 111
Baked Mediterranean Sea Bass with Roasted Vegetables 113
Grilled Mediterranean Mahi-Mahi Skewers with Pineapple Salsa..... 115
Mediterranean Tuna-Stuffed Tomatoes 117
Baked Mediterranean Salmon Cakes with Tzatziki Sauce................... 118
Grilled Mediterranean Swordfish and Vegetable Foil Packets 120
Mediterranean Baked Cod with Artichoke and Olive Tapenade........ 122
Mediterranean Shrimp Orzo Salad with Feta and Herbs 124

Grilled Mediterranean Snapper with Roasted Garlic Hummus 125
Roasted Garlic Hummus 126
Baked Mediterranean Halibut with Tomato-Basil Relish 127
Mediterranean Tuna Stuffed Avocado Boats 129
Grilled Mediterranean Salmon Skewers with Pesto Drizzle 130
Baked Mediterranean Cod with Roasted Red Pepper Sauce 132
Mediterranean Shrimp and Feta Stuffed Zucchini Boats 134

CHAPTER 4 SALADS, SIDES, AND VEGETARIAN DELIGHTS 137

Roasted Mediterranean Vegetable Medley 139
Mediterranean Quinoa and Vegetable Stuffed Portobello Mushrooms 141
Baked Mediterranean Ratatouille with Feta and Olives 143
Mediterranean Chickpea and Vegetable Salad 145
Grilled Mediterranean Vegetable Skewers with Zucchini Hummus 146
Baked Mediterranean Feta and Vegetable Stuffed Tomatoes 148
Mediterranean Roasted Vegetable and Farro Bowls 150
Grilled Mediterranean Veggie Burgers with Tzatziki Sauce 152
Baked Mediterranean Stuffed Zucchini Boats 154
Mediterranean Lentil and Vegetable Stew 156
Grilled Mediterranean Vegetable and Halloumi Skewers 158
Baked Mediterranean Eggplant Rollatini with Ricotta and Spinach 160
Mediterranean Roasted Cauliflower and Chickpea Salad 162
Grilled Mediterranean Vegetable and Feta Stuffed Portobello Mushrooms 164
Baked Mediterranean Vegetable Lasagna with Bechamel Sauce 166
Mediterranean Quinoa Stuffed Acorn Squash 168
Baked Mediterranean Feta and Spinach Stuffed Portobello Mushrooms 172
Mediterranean Roasted Vegetable and Orzo Salad 174
Grilled Mediterranean Vegetable and Halloumi Wraps with Hummus 176
Baked Mediterranean Stuffed Eggplant with Tomato-Basil Sauce 178
Mediterranean Roasted Vegetable and Feta Quinoa Bowls 180
Grilled Mediterranean Vegetable and Chickpea Skewers with Tahini Drizzle 182
Baked Mediterranean Zucchini Boats with Quinoa and Feta 184
Mediterranean Roasted Cauliflower and Lentil Salad 185

CHAPTER 5 FRESH AND FLAVORFUL FISH DISHES 187

Grilled Mediterranean Sea Bream with Lemon-Herb Marinade 189
Baked Cod with Tomato, Olive, and Caper Topping 190
Sautéed Shrimp and Zucchini Noodle Stir-Fry 191
Poached Salmon with Dill Yogurt Sauce 193

Mediterranean Tuna and White Bean Salad 195
Roasted Trout with Roasted Red Pepper Sauce 196
Baked Halibut with Fennel and Orange Salad 198
Grilled Swordfish Skewers with Pineapple Salsa 200
Mediterranean Mussels in White Wine Broth 202
Baked Stuffed Calamari with Herbed Breadcrumbs 204
Seared Scallops with Asparagus and Lemon Vinaigrette 206
Mediterranean Seafood Stew with Tomatoes and Herbs 208
Grilled Whole Branzino with Lemon and Herbs 210
Baked Salmon Cakes with Dill and Lemon 211
Sautéed Shrimp with Garlic, Lemon, and Parsley 213
Poached Tuna Salad with Olives and Roasted Peppers 214
Baked Cod with Tomato, Caper, and Olive Relish 216
Grilled Swordfish Steaks with Cucumber Salad 218
Mediterranean Baked Tilapia with Artichokes and Lemon 220
Seared Ahi Tuna with Avocado and Grapefruit Salad 222
Roasted Salmon with Mediterranean Quinoa Salad 224
Grilled Octopus with Lemon and Oregano 226
Baked Haddock with Tomato and Basil Topping 227
Sautéed Shrimp Scampi with Zucchini Noodles 228
Poached Halibut with Fennel and Orange Salsa 230

CHAPTER 6 DESSERTS AND BAKED TREATS 232

Mediterranean Lemon Olive Oil Cake 233
Baklava Bites 235
Pistachio and Honey Yogurt Parfaits 237
Baked Mediterranean Fig and Almond Stuffed Apples 238
Mediterranean Orange and Almond Biscotti 239
Grilled Mediterranean Fruit Skewers with Honey-Lemon Drizzle 241
Mediterranean Olive Oil and Rosemary Shortbread Cookies 242
Creamy Mediterranean Lemon Cheesecake Bars 244
Baked Mediterranean Ricotta and Honey Stuffed Figs 246
Mediterranean Almond and Orange Semolina Cake 247
Grilled Mediterranean Fruit Salad with Honey-Mint Syrup 249
Mediterranean Olive Oil and Sea Salt Chocolate Truffles 251
Baked Mediterranean Almond and Honey Stuffed Apricots 252
Mediterranean Lemon and Olive Oil Pound Cake 253
Grilled Mediterranean Fruit and Halloumi Skewers with Mint Yogurt Dip 255
Baked Mediterranean Pistachio and Date Baklava Rolls 257
Mediterranean Almond and Orange Blossom Water Meringues 259

Grilled Mediterranean Figs with Honey and Mascarpone 261
Baked Mediterranean Olive Oil and Sea Salt Shortbread Cookies 262
Mediterranean Lemon and Lavender Posset 263
Grilled Mediterranean Fruit and Halloumi Skewers with Pomegranate Molasses Glaze 264
Baked Mediterranean Almond and Honey Baklava Bites 266
Mediterranean Lemon and Olive Oil Ricotta Cake 268
Grilled Mediterranean Fruit and Mascarpone Stuffed Figs 270
Baked Mediterranean Pistachio and Orange Blossom Semolina Cake 271

CONCLUSION 273

INTRODUCTION

Dive into the world of wholesome eating with *Mediterranean Meal Prep for Beginners!* This comprehensive cookbook features 150 deliciously easy recipes that make embracing the Mediterranean diet both accessible and enjoyable. Perfect for novice cooks and busy individuals looking to infuse their meals with vibrant flavors and nourishing ingredients, this guide will transform how you approach meal prep. Inside, you'll discover:

- **150 Flavorful Recipes:** Each recipe is crafted with simplicity in mind, utilizing fresh, wholesome ingredients that highlight the rich culinary traditions of the Mediterranean. From zesty salads and hearty grain bowls to savory proteins and delightful snacks, there's a recipe for every palate.

- **Step-by-Step Instructions:** Clear, concise instructions ensure that even the most inexperienced cooks can create mouthwatering dishes. Enjoy the satisfaction of preparing healthy meals with confidence!

- **Meal Prep Made Easy:** Learn the essentials of meal prepping with practical tips on planning, shopping, and organizing your kitchen. Discover how to efficiently batch cook and store meals to save time during busy weekdays.

- **Nutritional Benefits:** Understand the health advantages of the Mediterranean diet, which emphasizes fresh vegetables, whole grains, healthy fats, and lean proteins. Each recipe is designed to nourish your body and support a balanced lifestyle.

- **Time-Saving Strategies:** Get insights on how to streamline your cooking process, making healthy eating a stress-free part of your daily routine. Enjoy the benefits of homemade meals without the hassle!

Whether you're looking to improve your health, explore new flavors, or simply save time in the kitchen, *Mediterranean Meal Prep for Beginners* is the ultimate resource for easy, healthy cooking. Embrace the joy of meal prepping and savor the delectable tastes of the Mediterranean every day! Start your culinary adventure today and make nourishing meals a delightful part of your life!

CHAPTER 1
BREAKFAST AND BRUNCH RECIPES

OVERNIGHT OATS WITH CHIA, HONEY, AND BERRIES

Total Prep Time: 10 minutes
Total Cooking Time: 0 minutes (overnight chilling)
Servings: 4

Ingredients:

- 1 cup (240ml) old-fashioned rolled oats
- 1/4 cup (60ml) chia seeds
- 2 cups (480ml) unsweetened almond milk (or milk of your choice)
- 2 tablespoons (30ml) honey, plus more for serving
- 1/2 teaspoon (2.5ml) vanilla extract
- 1/4 teaspoon (1.25ml) ground cinnamon
- 1 cup (150g) mixed berries (such as raspberries, blueberries, and/or blackberries)

Instructions:

1. To prepare the oat-chia mixture, combine rolled oats and chia seeds in a medium bowl and stir until thoroughly blended.
2. Add the almond milk, 2 tablespoons (30ml) of honey, vanilla extract, and ground cinnamon. Stir until all the ingredients are well incorporated.
3. Seal the bowl and place it in the refrigerator for at least 4 hours or overnight.
4. When ready to serve, give the overnight oats a stir. Spoon the oats into individual serving bowls or containers.
5. Top each serving with 1/4 cup (40g) of the mixed berries and drizzle with additional honey, if desired.

Nutritional breakdown per serving:

Calories: 250 kcal, Protein: 6 grams, Carbohydrates: 37 grams, Fat: 8 grams, Saturated Fat: 1 grams, Cholesterol: 0 milligrams, Sodium: 75 milligrams, Fiber: 8 grams, and Sugar: 4 grams.

SHAKSHUKA WITH FETA AND HERBS

Total Prep Time: 15 minutes
Total Cooking Time: 30 minutes
Servings: 4

Ingredients:

- 2 tablespoons (30ml) olive oil
- 1 onion, diced
- 1 red bell pepper, diced
- 3 garlic cloves, minced
- 1 teaspoon (5ml) ground cumin
- 1 teaspoon (5ml) paprika
- 1/2 teaspoon (2.5ml) crushed red pepper flakes (optional, for heat)
- 1 (28 oz or 800g) can crushed tomatoes
- 6 large eggs
- 1/2 cup (120g) crumbled feta cheese
- 2 tablespoons (30ml) chopped fresh parsley
- 2 tablespoons (30ml) chopped fresh cilantro
- Salt and black pepper, to taste
- Crusty bread, for serving

Instructions:

1. In a large skillet or ovenproof pan, heat the olive oil over medium heat. Sauté the diced onion and bell pepper for 5-7 minutes, or until softened.
2. Add the minced garlic, cumin, paprika, and crushed red pepper flakes (if using). Cook for 1 minute, stirring frequently, until aromatic.
3. Incorporate the can of crushed tomatoes into the pan and mix thoroughly until combined. Let the mixture simmer for 10-15 minutes, stirring occasionally, until the sauce thickens slightly.
4. Break the eggs directly into the tomato sauce, ensuring they are evenly spaced throughout the pan. Cover the pan tightly and cook for 8-10 minutes, or until the egg whites are cooked through but the yolks are still runny.
5. Sprinkle the dish with crumbled feta cheese, chopped parsley, and chopped cilantro. Finally, remove the pan from the heat.
6. Season with salt and pepper to taste.
7. Serve the Shakshuka immediately, with crusty bread on the side for dipping.

Nutritional breakdown per serving:

Calories: 590 kcal, Protein: 16 grams, Carbohydrates: 17 grams, Fat: 18 grams, Saturated Fat: 6 grams, Cholesterol: 320 milligrams, Sodium: 320 milligrams, Fiber: 4 grams, and Sugar: 6 grams.

MEDITERRANEAN VEGGIE FRITTATA

Total Prep Time: 20 minutes
Total Cooking Time: 25 minutes
Servings: 6

Ingredients:

- 8 large eggs
- 1/4 cup (60ml) unsweetened almond milk (or milk of your choice)
- 1/4 cup (60ml) crumbled feta cheese
- 2 tablespoons (30ml) chopped fresh basil
- 1 teaspoon (5ml) dried oregano
- Salt and black pepper, to taste
- 2 tablespoons (30ml) olive oil
- 1 red bell pepper, diced
- 1 zucchini, diced
- 1 cup (150g) cherry tomatoes, halved
- 1/2 cup (75g) kalamata olives, sliced
- 2 cloves garlic, minced
- 1/4 cup (60ml) grated Parmesan cheese

Instructions:

1. Get started by setting your oven temperature to 375°F (190°C).
2. In a large bowl, whisk together the eggs, almond milk, feta cheese, basil, and oregano. Season with salt and pepper to taste. Let cool.
3. Heat the olive oil in a 10-inch (25cm) oven-safe skillet over medium heat.
4. Add the diced red bell pepper, zucchini, cherry tomatoes, and sliced kalamata olives to the skillet. Sauté for 5-7 minutes, until the vegetables are slightly softened.
5. To the skillet, add the minced garlic. Cook for 1 minute until fragrant.
6. Evenly distribute the vegetables in the skillet. Then, pour the egg mixture over them.
7. Garnish the frittata with grated Parmesan cheese.
8. Bake the frittata in the preheated oven for 15-20 minutes, or until it is cooked through and the top is golden brown.
9. Let the frittata cool slightly for 5 minutes before slicing and serving.

Nutritional breakdown per serving:

Calories: 200 kcal, Protein: 13 grams, Carbohydrates: 8 grams, Fat: 14 grams, Saturated Fat: 4 grams, Cholesterol: 235 milligrams, Sodium: 450 milligrams, Fiber: 2 grams, and Sugar: 8 grams.

OLIVE OIL AND SEA SALT AVOCADO TOAST

Total Prep Time: 5 minutes
Total Cooking Time: 0 minutes
Servings: 2

Ingredients:

- 2 slices whole grain or sourdough bread
- 1 ripe avocado, halved and pitted
- 1 tablespoon (15ml) extra-virgin olive oil
- 1/4 teaspoon (1.25ml) flaky sea salt
- Freshly ground black pepper (optional)

Instructions:

1. Toast the bread slices to your desired level of doneness.
2. Scoop the flesh of the avocado halves into a small bowl and mash it with a fork, leaving it slightly chunky.
3. Divide the mashed avocado evenly between the two toasted bread slices, spreading it to the edges.
4. Drizzle 1/2 tablespoon (7.5ml) of extra-virgin olive oil over each slice of avocado toast.
5. Sprinkle 1/8 teaspoon (0.6ml) of flaky sea salt over each slice.
6. For extra flavor, add a few grinds of fresh black pepper.
7. Serve immediately and enjoy!

Nutritional breakdown per serving:

Calories: 260 kcal, Protein: 5 grams, Carbohydrates: 18 grams, Fat: 20 grams, Saturated Fat: 3 grams, Cholesterol: 0 milligrams, Sodium: 320 milligrams, Fiber: 8 grams, and Sugar: 5 grams.

GREEK YOGURT PARFAIT WITH GRANOLA AND POMEGRANATE

Total Prep Time: 10 minutes
Total Cooking Time: 0 minutes
Servings: 2

Ingredients:

- 1 cup (240g) plain Greek yogurt
- 1/2 cup (120ml) granola
- 1/2 cup (80g) pomegranate arils
- 1 tablespoon (15ml) honey (optional)

Instructions:

1. In two parfait glasses or small bowls, layer the ingredients in the following order:

   - 1/4 cup (60g) of Greek yogurt
   - 2 tablespoons (30ml) of granola
   - 1/4 cup (40g) of pomegranate arils

2. Repeat the layering process to create a second layer of each ingredient.

3. If desired, drizzle 1/2 tablespoon (7.5ml) of honey over the top of each parfait.

4. Serve immediately and enjoy!

Nutritional breakdown per serving:

Calories: 190 kcal, Protein: 13 grams, Carbohydrates: 26 grams, Fat: 5 grams, Saturated Fat: 1 grams, Cholesterol: 15 milligrams, Sodium: 45 milligrams, Fiber: 4 grams, and Sugar: 6 grams.

MEDITERRANEAN BREAKFAST BURRITO

Total Prep Time: 15 minutes
Total Cooking Time: 20 minutes
Servings: 4

Ingredients:

- 4 large eggs
- 2 tablespoons (30ml) water
- 1 tablespoon (15ml) olive oil
- 1/2 cup (75g) diced red bell pepper
- 1/2 cup (75g) diced zucchini
- 2 cloves garlic, minced
- 1/4 cup (60ml) crumbled feta cheese
- 2 tablespoons (30ml) chopped fresh parsley
- 4 whole wheat tortillas (8-inch/20cm diameter)
- Salt and black pepper, to taste

Instructions:

1. To prepare the egg mixture, whisk together eggs and water in a medium bowl until smooth. Season with salt and pepper.
2. To a large non-stick skillet, add a tablespoon of olive oil. Heat over medium-low heat.
3. To the pan, add the diced red bell pepper and zucchini. Sauté for 5-7 minutes until they become tender.
4. Sauté the minced garlic in the skillet for 1 minute, or until fragrant.
5. Pour the whisked eggs into the skillet and cook, stirring occasionally, until the eggs are scrambled and cooked through, about 3-5 minutes.
6. To the skillet, add crumbled feta cheese and chopped parsley. Stir to combine. Then, remove the skillet from the heat.
7. Warm the whole wheat tortillas according to the package instructions.
8. Evenly distribute the egg mixture among the 4 tortillas, placing it in the center of each.
9. To form a burrito, fold the bottom of the tortilla up over the filling. Fold the sides of the tortilla inward.
10. Serve the Mediterranean Breakfast Burritos immediately.

Nutritional breakdown per serving:

Calories: 320 kcal, Protein: 17 grams, Carbohydrates: 31 grams, Fat: 16 grams, Saturated Fat: 5 grams, Cholesterol: 190 milligrams, Sodium: 550 milligrams, Fiber: 5 grams, and Sugar: 8 grams.

BAKED OATMEAL WITH APPLES, CINNAMON, AND PECANS

Total Prep Time: 15 minutes
Total Cooking Time: 35 minutes
Servings: 6

Ingredients:

- 2 cups (180g) old-fashioned rolled oats
- 1/2 cup (100g) brown sugar
- 1 teaspoon (5ml) ground cinnamon
- 1/2 teaspoon (2.5ml) baking powder
- 1/4 teaspoon (1.25ml) salt
- 1 1/2 cups unsweetened almond milk
- 1 large egg
- 2 tablespoons (30ml) melted coconut oil or unsalted butter
- 1 teaspoon (5ml) vanilla extract
- 2 medium apples, peeled, cored, and chopped
- 1/2 cup (60g) chopped pecans

Instructions:

1. Get started by setting your oven temperature to 375°F (190°C). Grease an 8-inch (20cm) square baking dish.
2. Whisk together rolled oats, brown sugar, cinnamon, baking powder, and salt in a large bowl.
3. Combine almond milk, egg, melted coconut oil or butter, and vanilla extract in a separate bowl. Whisk until well blended.
4. Gently combine the wet and dry ingredients.
5. Gently incorporate the diced apples and pecans.
6. To the prepared baking dish, pour the mixture and spread it evenly.
7. Bake for 35-40 minutes, or until the top is golden brown and the oatmeal is set.
8. To the baked oatmeal, let it cool for 5 minutes before serving.
9. Serve warm and enjoy!

Nutritional breakdown per serving:

Calories: 290 kcal, Protein: 6 grams, Carbohydrates: 39 grams, Fat: 13 grams, Saturated Fat: 6 grams, Cholesterol: 35 milligrams, Sodium: 150 milligrams, Fiber: 5 grams, and Sugar: 2 grams.

SPINACH AND FETA STUFFED PORTOBELLO MUSHROOMS

Total Prep Time: 20 minutes
Total Cooking Time: 25 minutes
Servings: 4

Ingredients:

- 4 portobello mushroom caps, stems removed and chopped
- 2 tablespoons (30ml) olive oil, divided
- 1/2 cup (75g) diced onion
- 2 cloves garlic, minced
- 2 cups (60g) fresh spinach, chopped
- 1/2 cup (120g) crumbled feta cheese
- 2 tablespoons (30ml) grated Parmesan cheese
- 1/4 teaspoon (1.25ml) dried oregano
- 1/4 teaspoon (1.25ml) dried basil
- Salt and black pepper, to taste

Instructions:

1. Get started by setting your oven temperature to 400°F (200°C). Line a baking sheet with parchment paper.
2. Gently clean the portobello mushroom caps with a damp paper towel and remove the stems. Chop the stems.
3. In the skillet with the olive oil, combine the chopped mushroom stems, onion, and garlic. Sauté until the onion is translucent (about 5-7 minutes).
4. Sauté the chopped spinach in the skillet for 2-3 minutes, or until the spinach is wilted. Remove from heat and let cool slightly.
5. In a medium bowl, combine the sautéed mushroom stem mixture, feta cheese, Parmesan cheese, oregano, and basil. Season with salt and pepper to taste.
6. Brush the portobello caps with the remaining 1 tablespoon (15ml) of olive oil and place them on the prepared baking sheet, gill-side up.
7. Divide the spinach and feta filling evenly among the portobello caps, gently pressing it into the caps.
8. Cook in the oven for about 18 to 22 minutes, or until the filling is bubbling and the mushrooms have become tender.
9. Serve the Spinach and Feta Stuffed Portobello Mushrooms immediately.

Nutritional breakdown per serving:

Calories: 170 kcal, Protein: 9 grams, Carbohydrates: 9 grams, Fat: 12 grams, Saturated Fat: 4 grams, Cholesterol: 20 milligrams, Sodium: 420 milligrams, Fiber: 2 grams, and Sugar: 4 grams.

MEDITERRANEAN BREAKFAST BOWLS WITH QUINOA, EGGS, AND VEGGIES

Total Prep Time: 20 minutes
Total Cooking Time: 25 minutes
Servings: 4

Ingredients:

- 1 cup (185g) uncooked quinoa, rinsed
- 2 cups (480ml) vegetable or chicken broth
- 4 large eggs
- 2 tablespoons (30ml) olive oil
- 1/2 cup (75g) diced cucumber
- 1/2 cup (75g) diced tomatoes
- 1/4 cup (40g) diced red onion
- 2 tablespoons (30ml) chopped fresh parsley
- 2 tablespoons (30ml) crumbled feta cheese
- 1 tablespoon (15ml) lemon juice
- Salt and black pepper, to taste

Instructions:

1. In a medium-sized saucepan, mix the quinoa with the broth. Heat on high until it reaches a boil. After boiling, lower the heat, cover the pan, and let it simmer for 15 to 20 minutes, or until the quinoa is soft and the liquid has been fully absorbed.
2. As the quinoa cooks, warm a non-stick skillet on medium heat. Add the eggs to the skillet and cook for approximately 3 to 5 minutes, preparing them sunny-side up or over easy, until the whites are set and the yolks are still runny.
3. To each bowl, add a fried egg and sprinkle generously with crumbled feta cheese.
4. Drizzle the lemon juice and 1 tablespoon (15ml) of the olive oil over the quinoa mixture and toss gently to coat.
5. Season the quinoa mixture with salt and black pepper to taste.
6. Divide the quinoa mixture evenly among 4 bowls.
7. Top each bowl with a fried egg and sprinkle with the crumbled feta cheese.
8. Drizzle the remaining 1 tablespoon (15ml) of olive oil over the eggs.
9. Serve the Mediterranean Breakfast Bowls immediately.

Nutritional breakdown per serving:

Calories: 320 kcal, Protein: 14 grams, Carbohydrates: 32 grams, Fat: 16 grams, Saturated Fat: 4 grams, Cholesterol: 190 milligrams, Sodium: 430 milligrams, Fiber: 4 grams, and Sugar: 6 grams.

WHOLE WHEAT PANCAKES WITH BLUEBERRY COMPOTE

Total Prep Time: 20 minutes
Total Cooking Time: 20 minutes
Servings: 4 (4 pancakes per serving)

Ingredients:

Pancakes:

- 1 cup (120g) whole wheat flour
- 1 tablespoon (12g) granulated sugar
- 2 teaspoons (10ml) baking powder
- 1/2 teaspoon (2.5ml) baking soda
- 1/4 teaspoon (1.25ml) salt
- 1 cup (240ml) buttermilk
- 1 large egg
- 2 tablespoons (30ml) melted butter, plus more for griddle

Blueberry Compote:

- 1 cup (150g) fresh or frozen blueberries
- 2 tablespoons (30ml) maple syrup
- 1 tablespoon (15ml) lemon juice

Instructions:

Pancakes:

1. Combine whole wheat flour, sugar, baking powder, baking soda, and salt in a medium bowl. Whisk until well blended.
2. In a different bowl, combine the buttermilk, egg, and 2 tablespoons (30ml) of melted butter by whisking them together.
3. Stir the buttermilk mixture and dry ingredients together lightly until fully combined.
4. Warm a lightly greased griddle or non-stick frying pan over medium-high heat.
5. Cook for 2 to 3 minutes, or until bubbles form on the surface and the edges begin to appear dry.
6. Turn the pancakes over and cook for another 2 minutes, or until they achieve a golden-brown color.

7. To keep the cooked pancakes warm, place them in a preheated oven at 175°F (80°C) while you finish cooking the remaining batter.

Blueberry Compote:

1. In a small saucepan, mix together blueberries, maple syrup, and lemon juice.
2. Prepare the blueberry mixture over medium heat, stirring often, until the blueberries start to release their juices and the compote thickens, which should take around 5 to 7 minutes.
3. Take off the heat and allow it to cool for a moment before serving.

To Serve:

1. Place four pancakes on each plate and drizzle the warm blueberry compote on top.
2. Serve immediately.

Nutritional breakdown per serving:

Calories: 340 kcal, Protein: 10 grams, Carbohydrates: 49 grams, Fat: 12 grams, Saturated Fat: 6 grams, Cholesterol: 75 milligrams, Sodium: 510 milligrams, Fiber: 5 grams, and Sugar: 12 grams.

EGG AND VEGGIE STUFFED PITA POCKETS

Total Prep Time: 15 minutes
Total Cooking Time: 15 minutes
Servings: 4 (1 pita pocket per serving)

Ingredients:

- 4 whole wheat pita breads, halved
- 8 large eggs
- 1 tablespoon (15ml) olive oil
- 1/2 cup (75g) diced bell pepper
- 1/2 cup (75g) diced zucchini
- 1/4 cup (40g) diced red onion
- 2 tablespoons (30ml) chopped fresh parsley
- Salt and black pepper, to taste
- 2 tablespoons (30ml) crumbled feta cheese (optional)

Instructions:

1. In a spacious non-stick skillet, warm the olive oil over medium heat.
2. Scramble the eggs in the skillet, stirring continuously until fully cooked yet still tender (about 3-5 minutes).
3. Add the diced bell pepper, zucchini, and red onion to the scrambled eggs. Continue cooking for another 2 to 3 minutes, stirring from time to time, until the vegetables become tender.
4. Take the skillet off the heat and mix in the chopped parsley. Season the egg and vegetable mixture with salt and black pepper to taste.
5. Gently open each pita bread half and stuff it with the egg and vegetable mixture.
6. If desired, top each stuffed pita pocket with a sprinkle of crumbled feta cheese.
7. Serve the Egg and Veggie Stuffed Pita Pockets immediately.

Nutritional breakdown per serving:

Calories: 280 kcal, Protein: 17 grams, Carbohydrates: 26 grams, Fat: 13 grams, Saturated Fat: 3 grams, Cholesterol: 375 milligrams, Sodium: 460 milligrams, Fiber: 4 grams, and Sugar: 8 grams.

MEDITERRANEAN BREAKFAST SALAD WITH FARRO, EGGS, AND OLIVES

Total Prep Time: 20 minutes
Total Cooking Time: 25 minutes
Servings: 4

Ingredients:

- 1 cup (185g) dry farro, cooked according to package instructions
- 4 large eggs
- 1/2 cup (75g) cherry tomatoes, halved
- 1/2 cup (75g) sliced cucumber
- 1/4 cup (40g) pitted kalamata olives, halved
- 2 tablespoons (30ml) crumbled feta cheese
- 2 tablespoons (30ml) chopped fresh parsley
- 1 tablespoon (15ml) olive oil
- 1 tablespoon (15ml) red wine vinegar
- Salt and black pepper, to taste

Instructions:

1. Prepare the farro by following the instructions on the package. After cooking, drain it and let it cool for a short while.
2. In a medium saucepan, bring water to a rolling boil. Gently add the eggs and let them cook for 6 to 7 minutes to achieve soft-boiled eggs. Once done, drain the eggs and allow them to cool for a bit.
3. In a spacious bowl, mix together the cooked farro, cherry tomatoes cut in half, sliced cucumber, halved kalamata olives, crumbled feta cheese, and chopped parsley.
4. Sprinkle the salad with olive oil and red wine vinegar, then carefully toss to evenly distribute the dressing.
5. Adjust the seasoning of the salad with salt and black pepper according to your taste.
6. Peel the soft-boiled eggs and cut them in half.
7. Divide the salad evenly among 4 bowls or plates. Top each serving with 2 soft-boiled egg halves.
8. Serve the Mediterranean Breakfast Salad immediately.

Nutritional breakdown per serving:

Calories: 320 kcal, Protein: 16 grams, Carbohydrates: 35 grams, Fat: 14 grams, Saturated Fat: 4 grams, Cholesterol: 215 milligrams, Sodium: 480 milligrams, Fiber: 6 grams, and Sugar: 5 grams.

BAKED EGGS IN TOMATO CUPS WITH BASIL AND PARMESAN

Total Prep Time: 15 minutes
Total Cooking Time: 25 minutes
Servings: 4 (1 stuffed tomato per serving)

Ingredients:

- 4 medium-sized tomatoes
- 4 large eggs
- 2 tablespoons (30ml) grated Parmesan cheese
- 2 tablespoons (30ml) chopped fresh basil, plus more for garnish
- 1 tablespoon (15ml) olive oil
- Salt and black pepper, to taste

Instructions:

1. Get started by setting your oven temperature to 375°F (190°C).
2. Remove the tops of the tomatoes and use a spoon to hollow them out, ensuring a shell that is 1/4-inch (6mm) thick. Dice the removed tomato flesh and set it aside for later use.
3. Arrange the tomato shells in a baking dish or on a baking sheet.
4. Mix the diced tomato pulp, shredded Parmesan cheese, and chopped basil together in a small bowl.
5. Crack one egg into each tomato shell, being careful not to break the yolk.
6. Spoon the tomato-Parmesan mixture evenly over the eggs, making sure the egg yolks are still visible.
7. Garnish the stuffed tomato cups with a drizzle of olive oil.
8. Season the stuffed tomatoes with salt and black pepper to taste.
9. Bake until the egg whites are firm and the yolks reach your desired doneness, which should take approximately 20 to 25 minutes.
10. Remove the baked tomato cups from the oven and let them cool for a few minutes.
11. Garnish the Baked Eggs in Tomato Cups with additional chopped fresh basil before serving.

Nutritional breakdown per serving:

Calories: 150 kcal, Protein: 9 grams, Carbohydrates: 9 grams, Fat: 9 grams, Saturated Fat: 2.5 grams, Cholesterol: 190 milligrams, Sodium: 220 milligrams, Fiber: 2 grams, and Sugar: 5 grams.

TROPICAL CHIA SEED PUDDING WITH MANGO AND COCONUT MILK

Total Prep Time: 10 minutes
Total Chilling Time: 4 hours or overnight
Servings: 4

Ingredients:

- 1/2 cup (120ml) unsweetened coconut milk
- 1/2 cup (120ml) unsweetened almond milk
- 3 tablespoons (45ml) chia seeds
- 2 tablespoons (30ml) maple syrup
- 1 teaspoon (5ml) vanilla extract
- 1 cup (150g) diced fresh mango
- 2 tablespoons (30ml) shredded unsweetened coconut, for garnish

Instructions:

1. In a medium-sized bowl, thoroughly whisk together coconut milk, almond milk, chia seeds, maple syrup, and vanilla extract until everything is well blended.
2. Cover the bowl and refrigerate the chia seed pudding for at least 4 hours or overnight, stirring occasionally, until thickened.
3. When ready to serve, divide the chia seed pudding evenly among 4 serving bowls or cups.
4. Top each portion of chia seed pudding with 1/4 cup (37.5g) of diced fresh mango.
5. Sprinkle the chia seed pudding with the shredded unsweetened coconut.
6. Serve the Chia Seed Pudding with Mango and Coconut Milk chilled.

Nutritional breakdown per serving:

Calories: 170 kcal, Protein: 4 grams, Carbohydrates: 20 grams, Fat: 9 grams, Saturated Fat: 6 grams, Cholesterol: 0 milligrams, Sodium: 35 milligrams, Fiber: 5 grams, and Sugar: 3 grams.

MEDITERRANEAN BREAKFAST SKILLET WITH SAUSAGE AND ROASTED VEGGIES

Total Prep Time: 20 minutes
Total Cooking Time: 40 minutes
Servings: 4

Ingredients:

- 1 medium zucchini, diced
- 1 red bell pepper, diced
- 1 cup (150g) cherry tomatoes, halved
- 1 red onion, diced
- 3 cloves garlic, minced
- 2 tablespoons (30ml) olive oil
- Salt and black pepper, to taste
- 4 links (400g) cooked Mediterranean-style chicken or turkey sausage, sliced
- 6 large eggs
- 1/4 cup (40g) crumbled feta cheese
- 2 tablespoons (30ml) chopped fresh parsley

Instructions:

1. Get started by setting your oven temperature to 400°F (200°C).
2. In a spacious oven-safe skillet or baking dish, combine the diced zucchini, bell pepper, cherry tomatoes, red onion, and minced garlic. Add salt and pepper for seasoning, followed by a drizzle of olive oil. Mix thoroughly to make sure all ingredients are evenly coated.
3. To the preheated oven, add the vegetables. Cook in the oven for 20 to 25 minutes, making sure to stir halfway through, until the vegetables are soft and exhibit a light brown color.
4. Add the sliced sausage to the skillet containing the roasted vegetables and stir thoroughly to blend the ingredients.
5. In the vegetable and sausage mixture, create six indentations. Carefully crack an egg into each one.
6. Return the skillet to the oven and bake for an additional 8-10 minutes, or until the egg whites are set and the yolks are cooked to your desired doneness.
7. Remove the Mediterranean Breakfast Skillet from the oven and sprinkle the crumbled feta cheese and chopped parsley over the top.

8. Serve the skillet warm, either directly from the oven or after allowing it to cool slightly.

Nutritional breakdown per serving:

Calories: 390 kcal, Protein: 28 grams, Carbohydrates: 18 grams, Fat: 24 grams, Saturated Fat: 7 grams, Cholesterol: 330 milligrams, Sodium: 800 milligrams, Fiber: 4 grams, and Sugar: 9 grams.

ZUCCHINI FRITTERS WITH TZATZIKI DIPPING SAUCE

Total Prep Time: 20 minutes
Total Cooking Time: 15 minutes
Servings: 4 (4 fritters per serving)

Ingredients:

Zucchini Fritters:

- 2 medium zucchini, grated
- 1/2 cup (60g) all-purpose flour
- 2 large eggs, beaten
- 1/4 cup (40g) crumbled feta cheese
- 2 tablespoons (30ml) chopped fresh dill
- 1 tablespoon (15ml) lemon juice
- 1/2 teaspoon (2.5ml) baking powder
- Salt and black pepper, to taste
- 2 tablespoons (30ml) olive oil for frying

Tzatziki Dipping Sauce:

- 1 cup (240ml) plain Greek yogurt
- 1/2 cucumber, peeled, seeded, chopped
- 1 garlic clove, minced
- 1 tablespoon (15ml) lemon juice
- 2 tablespoons (30ml) chopped fresh dill
- Salt and black pepper, to taste

Instructions:

Zucchini Fritters:

1. To the grated zucchini, apply pressure with a clean kitchen towel or cheesecloth to remove the excess moisture.
2. In a medium bowl, mix the grated zucchini, flour, beaten eggs, feta cheese, chopped dill, lemon juice, baking powder, salt, and black pepper until well combined.
3. To a large skillet, add olive oil. Heat over medium heat.

4. Scoop heaping tablespoons of the zucchini mixture and gently place them in the hot oil, flattening them slightly with a spatula. Fry the fritters until golden brown (about 2-3 minutes per side).
5. Transfer the cooked zucchini fritters to a paper towel-lined plate to drain any excess oil.

Tzatziki Dipping Sauce:

1. In another bowl, combine the Greek yogurt, chopped cucumber, minced garlic, lemon juice, diced dill, salt, and black pepper. Mix thoroughly until the ingredients are evenly blended.
2. Serve the Zucchini Fritters warm with the Tzatziki Dipping Sauce on the side.

Nutritional breakdown per serving:

Calories: 280 kcal, Protein: 15 grams, Carbohydrates: 18 grams, Fat: 17 grams, Saturated Fat: 5 grams, Cholesterol: 115 milligrams, Sodium: 410 milligrams, Fiber: 3 grams, and Sugar: 4 grams.

LENTIL AND EGG BREAKFAST BOWL WITH FETA AND OLIVES

Total Prep Time: 15 minutes
Total Cooking Time: 20 minutes
Servings: 4

Ingredients:

- 1 cup (200g) cooked brown or green lentils
- 4 large eggs
- 1/4 cup (40g) crumbled feta cheese
- 1/4 cup (35g) pitted and sliced Kalamata olives
- 2 tablespoons (30ml) extra-virgin olive oil
- 1 garlic clove, minced
- 1 teaspoon (5ml) lemon juice
- 2 tablespoons (30ml) chopped fresh parsley
- Salt and black pepper, to taste

Instructions:

1. To a medium saucepan, add olive oil. Heat over medium heat. Introduce the minced garlic and sauté for one minute, stirring occasionally, until it becomes aromatic.
2. Incorporate the cooked lentils into the saucepan, mixing them with the garlic and olive oil. Allow the lentils to heat for approximately 2-3 minutes.
3. Crack the eggs directly into the saucepan with the lentils, spacing them out evenly. Place a lid on the saucepan and let it cook for 4-6 minutes, or until the egg whites are firm and the yolks reach your preferred level of doneness.
4. Take the saucepan off the heat and gently spoon the lentil and egg combination into four separate serving bowls.
5. Top each bowl with crumbled feta cheese, sliced Kalamata olives, a drizzle of lemon juice, and chopped fresh parsley.
6. Season the Lentil and Egg Breakfast Bowls with salt and black pepper to taste.
7. Serve the Lentil and Egg Breakfast Bowls warm.

Nutritional breakdown per serving:

Calories: 270 kcal, Protein: 16 grams, Carbohydrates: 19 grams, Fat: 15 grams, Saturated Fat: 4 grams, Cholesterol: 215 milligrams, Sodium: 570 milligrams, Fiber: 7 grams, and Sugar: 6 grams.

MEDITERRANEAN BREAKFAST QUICHE WITH SPINACH AND FETA

Total Prep Time: 20 minutes
Total Cooking Time: 45 minutes
Servings: 6

Ingredients:

Crust:

- 1 1/4 cups (155g) all-purpose flour
- 1/2 teaspoon (2.5ml) salt
- 1/2 cup (115g) unsalted butter, chilled and cubed
- 3-4 tablespoons (45-60ml) ice water

Filling:

- 1 tablespoon (15ml) olive oil
- 1 small onion, diced
- 3 garlic cloves, minced
- 5 cups (150g) fresh spinach, chopped
- 6 large eggs
- 1 cup (240ml) milk
- 1/2 cup (120ml) heavy cream
- 1/2 teaspoon (2.5ml) dried oregano
- 1/4 teaspoon (1.25ml) red pepper flakes (optional)
- Salt and black pepper, to taste
- 1 cup (120g) crumbled feta cheese

Instructions:

Crust:

1. Incorporate flour and salt into a food processor. Pulse with chilled butter cubes until the mixture has a coarse crumb-like consistency.
2. Slowly add the ice water, measuring one tablespoon at a time, and pulse the mixture until the dough starts to take shape.

3. Move the dough onto a surface that has been floured and mold it into a disc. Next, encase it in plastic wrap and place it in the refrigerator for a minimum of 30 minutes.
4. Get started by setting your oven temperature to 375°F (190°C).
5. Lightly flour a surface and then roll the dough out into a circle that measures 12 inches across. Gently move the dough to a 9-inch pie dish, pressing it down into the base and along the sides. Remove any extra dough from the edges.
6. Use a fork to poke holes in the bottom of the crust, then bake it for 15 minutes. Remove from the oven and let cool.

Filling:

1. In a spacious skillet, warm the olive oil over medium heat. Incorporate the chopped onion and minced garlic, cooking for 2-3 minutes until they become tender.
2. Add the chopped spinach and sauté until it wilts, which will take about 2-3 minutes. Afterward, remove it from the heat and let it cool briefly.
3. In a large mixing bowl, blend the eggs, milk, heavy cream, dried oregano, salt, black pepper, and red pepper flakes (if you choose to use them). Whisk the mixture thoroughly until everything is combined.
4. Drizzle the egg mixture on top, then evenly distribute the crumbled feta cheese over it.
5. Bake the quiche for 30-35 minutes, or until the center is set and the top is lightly golden.
6. Give the quiche a 10-minute cooling period before you slice and serve it.

Nutritional breakdown per serving:

Calories: 370 kcal, Protein: 15 grams, Carbohydrates: 19 grams, Fat: 26 grams, Saturated Fat: 13 grams, Cholesterol: 230 milligrams, Sodium: 610 milligrams, Fiber: 2 grams, and Sugar: 2 grams.

BAKED OATMEAL CUPS WITH APRICOTS AND ALMONDS

Total Prep Time: 15 minutes
Total Cooking Time: 30 minutes
Servings: 12 cups

Ingredients:

- 2 cups (180g) old-fashioned rolled oats
- 1/2 cup (100g) brown sugar
- 1 teaspoon (5ml) baking powder
- 1/2 teaspoon (2.5ml) ground cinnamon
- 1/4 teaspoon (1.25ml) salt
- 1 1/4 cups (295ml) milk
- 1 large egg
- 2 tablespoons (30ml) unsalted butter, melted
- 1 teaspoon (5ml) vanilla extract
- 1 cup (150g) diced fresh or dried apricots
- 1/3 cup (50g) slivered almonds

Instructions:

1. Get started by setting your oven temperature to 375°F (190°C). To prepare a 12-cup muffin tin, grease or line it with paper liners.
2. In a large bowl, blend the rolled oats, brown sugar, baking powder, cinnamon, and salt, making sure that all the ingredients are fully combined.
3. To a different bowl, add milk, egg, melted butter, and vanilla extract. Whisk until fully combined.
4. Combine the wet and dry ingredients. Stir gently until just combined..
5. Fold in the diced apricots and slivered almonds.
6. Divide the oatmeal mixture evenly among the prepared muffin cups, filling them about 3/4 full.
7. Put in the oven and bake for 25 to 30 minutes, or until the tops turn a golden brown and a toothpick inserted into the center emerges clean.
8. Give the baked oatmeal cups 5 minutes to rest in the muffin tin, then move them to a wire rack to cool thoroughly.

Nutritional breakdown per serving:

Calories: 180 kcal, Protein: 5 grams, Carbohydrates: 28 grams, Fat: 6 grams, Saturated Fat: 2 grams, Cholesterol: 25 milligrams, Sodium: 110 milligrams, Fiber: 3 grams, and Sugar: 3 grams.

MEDITERRANEAN BREAKFAST SANDWICHES WITH ROASTED RED PEPPER SPREAD

Total Prep Time: 20 minutes
Total Cooking Time: 25 minutes
Servings: 4 sandwiches

Ingredients:

Roasted Red Pepper Spread:

- 1 red bell pepper
- 2 tablespoons (30ml) olive oil
- 2 tablespoons (30ml) Kalamata olives, pitted and chopped
- 2 tablespoons (30ml) crumbled feta cheese
- 1 garlic clove, minced
- 1 tablespoon (15ml) lemon juice
- Salt and black pepper, to taste

Sandwich Assembly:

- 4 whole wheat English muffins, halved
- 4 large eggs, cooked to your preference (fried, scrambled, or poached)
- 4 slices tomato
- 4 leaves fresh spinach or arugula
- 4 slices cucumber

Instructions:

Roasted Red Pepper Spread:

1. Get started by setting your oven temperature to 400°F (200°C).
2. Arrange the entire red bell pepper on a baking sheet and roast for 20 to 25 minutes, turning it from time to time until the skin is charred and blistered.
3. Take the pepper out of the oven and set it in a bowl. Wrap it in plastic and let it steam for 10 minutes.
4. Remove the skin from the pepper, discard the seeds and membranes, then chop the flesh of the pepper.
5. In a small bowl, mix together the diced roasted red pepper, olive oil, Kalamata olives, feta cheese, garlic, and lemon juice. Incorporate salt and black pepper to taste.

Sandwich Assembly:

1. Toast the English muffin halves until lightly golden.
2. Spread a generous amount of the roasted red pepper spread on the bottom half of each English muffin.
3. Top each muffin bottom with one cooked egg, one slice of tomato, one leaf of spinach or arugula, and one slice of cucumber.
4. Place the top half of the English muffin on each sandwich and serve immediately.

Nutritional breakdown per serving:

Calories: 320 kcal, Protein: 15 grams, Carbohydrates: 30 grams, Fat: 17 grams, Saturated Fat: 4 grams, Cholesterol: 215 milligrams, Sodium: 610 milligrams, Fiber: 5 grams, and Sugar: 2 grams.

YOGURT, GRANOLA, AND FRUIT PARFAIT JARS

Total Prep Time: 10 minutes
Total Cooking Time: 0 minutes
Servings: 4 parfait jars

Ingredients:

- 2 cups (480ml) plain Greek yogurt
- 1 1/2 cups (240g) granola
- 2 cups (300g) mixed fresh fruit (such as strawberries, blueberries, raspberries)
- 1 tablespoon (15ml) honey (optional)

Instructions:

1. Divide the plain Greek yogurt evenly among 4 Mason jars or small glasses.
2. Top each layer of yogurt with a layer of granola.
3. Place a layer of assorted fresh fruit over the granola.
4. Repeat the layers of yogurt, granola, and fruit, ending with the fruit.
5. If desired, drizzle a teaspoon (5ml) of honey over the top of each parfait.
6. Secure the lids on the Mason jars or cover the glasses with plastic wrap or lids.
7. Refrigerate the parfait jars until ready to serve, or up to 3 days.
8. Before serving, give each jar a gentle stir to combine the layers.

Nutritional breakdown per serving:

Calories: 250 kcal, Protein: 15 grams, Carbohydrates: 40 grams, Fat: 5 grams, Saturated Fat: 1 grams, Cholesterol: 15 milligrams, Sodium: 80 milligrams, Fiber: 5 grams, and Sugar: 1 grams.

CHICKPEA AND VEGETABLE BREAKFAST HASH

Total Prep Time: 15 minutes
Total Cooking Time: 25 minutes
Servings: 4

Ingredients:

- 1 (15.5 oz / 440g) can chickpeas, drained and rinsed
- 2 tablespoons (30ml) olive oil
- 1 medium onion, diced
- 1 red bell pepper, diced
- 2 cups (300g) diced sweet potato or yukon gold potato
- 2 cloves garlic, minced
- 1 teaspoon (5ml) smoked paprika
- 1/2 teaspoon (2.5ml) ground cumin
- Salt and black pepper, to taste
- 4 large eggs
- 2 tablespoons (30ml) chopped fresh parsley (optional)

Instructions:

1. To a large skillet, add olive oil. Heat over medium heat.
2. Add the diced onion, bell pepper, and diced potato to the skillet. Stirring occasionally, cook the vegetables for about 8 to 10 minutes, or until they become tender and develop a light brown color.
3. In the skillet, combine the rinsed and drained chickpeas with minced garlic, smoked paprika, and cumin. Stir thoroughly and cook for an additional 2 to 3 minutes to ensure the chickpeas are completely heated.
4. Season the hash with salt and black pepper to taste.
5. Form four small pockets in the hash mixture and gently break the eggs into each of these indentations.
6. Place a lid on the skillet and cook for 5 to 7 minutes, or until the eggs reach your preferred level of doneness.
7. Take the skillet off the heat and, if you like, sprinkle the hash with freshly chopped parsley for garnish.
8. Serve the Chickpea and Vegetable Breakfast Hash immediately, while the eggs are still warm.

Nutritional breakdown per serving:

Calories: 320 kcal, Protein: 15 grams, Carbohydrates: 39 grams, Fat: 12 grams, Saturated Fat: 2 grams, Cholesterol: 185 milligrams, Sodium: 380 milligrams, Fiber: 8 grams, and Sugar: 2 grams.

SPINACH AND FETA BREAKFAST WRAPS

Total Prep Time: 15 minutes
Total Cooking Time: 15 minutes
Servings: 4 wraps

Ingredients:

- 4 large eggs
- 2 tablespoons (30ml) milk
- 1/4 teaspoon (1.25ml) salt
- 1/8 teaspoon (0.6ml) black pepper
- 1 tablespoon (15ml) olive oil
- 2 cups (60g) fresh spinach, roughly chopped
- 1/4 cup (60g) crumbled feta cheese
- 4 whole wheat tortillas or wraps

Instructions:

1. To a medium bowl, add eggs, milk, salt, and pepper. Whisk until well combined.
2. To a nonstick skillet, add olive oil. Heat over medium heat.
3. To the skillet, pour the whisked eggs. Scramble the eggs until cooked through (about 3-5 minutes). Stir occasionally.
4. Add the chopped spinach to the scrambled eggs and cook for an additional 1-2 minutes, until the spinach is wilted.
5. Sprinkle crumbled feta cheese over the dish. Remove the pan from the heat.
6. Lay the whole wheat tortillas or wraps on a flat surface. Divide the spinach and feta egg mixture evenly among the tortillas, spreading it down the center of each wrap.
7. First, lift the bottom of the tortilla over the filling. After that, fold the sides inward and roll it up snugly to shape your wrap.
8. Serve the Spinach and Feta Breakfast Wraps immediately.

Nutritional breakdown per serving:

Calories: 250 kcal, Protein: 15 grams, Carbohydrates: 22 grams, Fat: 12 grams, Saturated Fat: 4 grams, Cholesterol: 195 milligrams, Sodium: 550 milligrams, Fiber: 4 grams, and Sugar: 2 grams.

BAKED EGGS IN TOMATO SAUCE WITH OLIVES AND FETA

Total Prep Time: 15 minutes
Total Cooking Time: 25 minutes
Servings: 4

Ingredients:

- 1 tablespoon (15ml) olive oil
- 1 small onion, diced
- 3 cloves garlic, minced
- 1 (14.5 oz / 411g) can diced tomatoes
- 1/2 cup (120ml) tomato sauce
- 1/4 cup (60ml) vegetable or chicken broth
- 1 teaspoon (5ml) dried oregano
- 1/4 teaspoon (1.25ml) red pepper flakes (optional)
- Salt and black pepper, to taste
- 4 large eggs
- 1/4 cup (60g) crumbled feta cheese
- 1/4 cup (40g) pitted black olives, sliced

Instructions:

1. Get started by setting your oven temperature to 375°F (190°C).
2. Place a 10-inch skillet or baking dish that is suitable for the oven on medium heat and allow the olive oil to warm up.
3. Add the diced onion and sauté for 3-4 minutes, until translucent.
4. Incorporate the minced garlic and sauté for another minute, or until it becomes aromatic.
5. Add the diced tomatoes, tomato sauce, and broth to the mixture. Mix in the dried oregano and red pepper flakes, if desired. Modify the seasoning with salt and black pepper based on your personal taste.
6. Cook the mixture over a simmer for 5 to 7 minutes, occasionally stirring, until the sauce starts to thicken.
7. Use the back of a spoon to make 4 small wells in the tomato sauce. Crack one egg into each well.
8. Add crumbled feta cheese and sliced black olives as a garnish on the dish.

9. Place the skillet or baking dish into the preheated oven and bake for 12 to 15 minutes, making sure the egg whites are thoroughly cooked while keeping the yolks runny.
10. Serve the Baked Eggs in Tomato Sauce with Olives and Feta immediately, while hot.

Nutritional breakdown per serving:

Calories: 210 kcal, Protein: 12 grams, Carbohydrates: 12 grams, Fat: 13 grams, Saturated Fat: 4 grams, Cholesterol: 190 milligrams, Sodium: 730 milligrams, Fiber: 3 grams, and Sugar: 2 grams.

BREAKFAST QUINOA BOWL WITH FIGS, NUTS, AND HONEY

Total Prep Time: 10 minutes
Total Cooking Time: 20 minutes
Servings: 4

Ingredients:

- 1 cup (185g) uncooked quinoa, rinsed
- 2 cups (475ml) unsweetened almond milk (or milk of your choice)
- 1/4 teaspoon (1.25ml) ground cinnamon
- 1/8 teaspoon (0.6ml) ground nutmeg
- 1/4 cup (40g) chopped dried figs
- 1/4 cup (35g) chopped toasted walnuts or almonds
- 2 tablespoons (30ml) honey
- 2 tablespoons (30ml) Greek yogurt (optional)

Instructions:

1. In a medium saucepan, mix the rinsed quinoa with almond milk. Heat the mixture over high heat until it reaches a boil.
2. To the boiling mixture, reduce heat and cover the saucepan. Allow the quinoa to cook for 15 to 18 minutes, until it becomes tender and all the liquid has been absorbed.
3. Take the saucepan off the heat and mix in the ground cinnamon and nutmeg.
4. Divide the cooked quinoa evenly among 4 serving bowls.
5. Top each bowl of quinoa with chopped dried figs, chopped toasted nuts, and a drizzle of honey.
6. If you prefer, add a spoonful of Greek yogurt to each bowl before serving.

Nutritional breakdown per serving:

Calories: 280 kcal, Protein: 8 grams, Carbohydrates: 44 grams, Fat: 9 grams, Saturated Fat: 1 grams, Cholesterol: 0 milligrams, Sodium: 50 milligrams, Fiber: 5 grams, and Sugar: 2 grams.

CHAPTER 2
DELICIOUS LUNCH AND DINNER IDEAS

MEDITERRANEAN CHICKPEA AND TUNA SALAD

Total Prep Time: 15 minutes
Total Cooking Time: 0 minutes
Servings: 4 (1 cup per serving)

Ingredients:

- 1 (15-ounce or 425g) can chickpeas, rinsed and drained
- 1 (5-ounce or 142g) can tuna, drained
- 1/2 cup (80g) diced cucumber
- 1/4 cup (40g) diced red onion
- 2 tablespoons (10g) chopped fresh parsley
- 2 tablespoons (10g) chopped fresh basil
- 2 tablespoons (30ml) lemon juice
- 1 tablespoon (15ml) olive oil
- 1 clove garlic, minced
- 1/4 teaspoon (1.25ml) dried oregano
- Salt and black pepper to taste

Instructions:

1. In a spacious bowl, mix together rinsed and drained chickpeas, drained tuna, diced cucumber, red onion, and chopped fresh parsley and basil.
2. In a small bowl, create a vinaigrette by whisking together lemon juice, olive oil, minced garlic, and dried oregano.
3. Add the dressing to the chickpea and tuna mixture and stir gently until evenly coated.
4. Season the Mediterranean Chickpea and Tuna Salad with salt and black pepper to taste.
5. Serve the salad according to your preference: chilled or at room temperature.

Nutritional breakdown per serving:

Calories: 190 kcal, Protein: 15 grams, Carbohydrates: 16 grams, Fat: 7 grams, Saturated Fat: 1 grams, Cholesterol: 20 milligrams, Sodium: 410 milligrams, Fiber: 5 grams, and Sugar: 4 grams.

ROASTED BEET AND FARRO SALAD WITH GOAT CHEESE

Total Prep Time: 25 minutes
Total Cooking Time: 45 minutes
Servings: 4

Ingredients:

- 3 medium beets, peeled and cut into 1-inch cubes
- 2 tablespoons (30ml) olive oil, divided
- Salt and black pepper to taste
- 1 cup (185g) dry farro, cooked according to package instructions
- 4 ounces (115g) crumbled goat cheese
- 1/4 cup (40g) chopped toasted walnuts
- 3 tablespoons (45ml) balsamic vinegar
- 1 tablespoon (15ml) Dijon mustard
- 1 tablespoon (15ml) honey
- 1 clove garlic, minced
- 2 cups (60g) baby arugula

Instructions:

1. Get started by setting your oven temperature to 400°F (200°C).
2. Toss the cubed beets with 1 tablespoon (15ml) of olive oil on a baking sheet. Season with salt and black pepper.
3. Roast the beets for 35-45 minutes, or until they are tender and lightly caramelized. Allow to cool slightly.
4. In a large bowl, mix roasted beets, cooked farro, crumbled goat cheese, and chopped toasted walnuts.
5. Create a dressing by whisking together the remaining olive oil, balsamic vinegar, Dijon mustard, honey, and garlic in a small bowl. Adjust the seasoning of the dressing with salt and black pepper to taste.
6. Pour the dressing over the beet and farro mixture and toss gently to coat.
7. Add the baby arugula to the salad and toss again to combine.
8. Serve the Roasted Beet and Farro Salad with Goat Cheese chilled or at room temperature.

Nutritional breakdown per serving:

Calories: 330 kcal, Protein: 11 grams, Carbohydrates: 37 grams, Fat: 17 grams, Saturated Fat: 5 grams, Cholesterol: 15 milligrams, Sodium: 370 milligrams, Fiber: 6 grams, and Sugar: 10 grams.

GRILLED ZUCCHINI AND FETA SALAD WITH LEMON HERB DRESSING

Total Prep Time: 20 minutes
Total Cooking Time: 15 minutes
Servings: 4

Ingredients:

- 3 medium zucchini, sliced lengthwise into 1/2-inch thick strips
- 2 tablespoons olive oil, extra for brushing
- Salt and black pepper to taste
- 4 ounces (115g) crumbled feta cheese
- 1/4 cup (40g) chopped fresh parsley
- 2 tablespoons (10g) chopped fresh mint
- 2 tablespoons (30ml) lemon juice
- 1 tablespoon (15ml) red wine vinegar
- 1 teaspoon (5ml) Dijon mustard
- 1 clove garlic, minced
- 1/4 cup (60ml) extra virgin olive oil

Instructions:

1. Get the grill or grill pan hot, medium-high heat.
2. Brush the zucchini slices lightly with olive oil and season with salt and black pepper.
3. Grill zucchini 3-4 minutes per side or until tender and charred. Cool slightly, then chop into 1-inch pieces.
4. Toss the grilled zucchini, crumbled feta, chopped parsley, and mint together in a large bowl.
5. Create a dressing by whisking together lemon juice, red wine vinegar, Dijon mustard, finely chopped garlic, and 60ml extra virgin olive oil in a small bowl. Enhance the dressing with salt and pepper according to your preference.
6. Pour the lemon herb dressing over the zucchini and feta salad, and toss gently to coat.
7. Serve the Grilled Zucchini and Feta Salad with Lemon Herb Dressing chilled or at room temperature.

Nutritional breakdown per serving:

Calories: 260 kcal, Protein: 8 grams, Carbohydrates: 12 grams, Fat: 21 grams, Saturated Fat: 6 grams, Cholesterol: 25 milligrams, Sodium: 470 milligrams, Fiber: 3 grams, and Sugar: 5 grams.

MEDITERRANEAN QUINOA AND CUCUMBER SALAD WITH DILL

Total Prep Time: 20 minutes
Total Cooking Time: 15 minutes
Servings: 4

Ingredients:

- 1 cup (185g) dry quinoa, cooked according to package instructions and cooled
- 1 English cucumber, diced (about 2 cups)
- 1/2 cup (80g) diced red onion
- 1/2 cup (80g) diced bell pepper
- 1/4 cup (10g) chopped fresh dill
- 2 tablespoons (10g) chopped fresh parsley
- 2 tablespoons (30ml) lemon juice
- 1 tablespoon (15ml) olive oil
- 1 clove garlic, minced
- 1/4 teaspoon (1.25ml) ground cumin
- Salt and black pepper to taste

Instructions:

1. In a spacious bowl, combine the chilled cooked quinoa with diced cucumber, red onion, bell pepper, and finely chopped dill and parsley.
2. Create a dressing by whisking lemon juice, olive oil, minced garlic, and cumin in a small bowl. Season to taste with salt and pepper.
3. Blend the dressing into the quinoa and vegetable mixture with a light toss.
4. For optimal flavor, chill the Mediterranean Quinoa and Cucumber Salad in the refrigerator for 10 minutes or more before serving.
5. This salad can be served chilled or brought to room temperature before serving.

Nutritional breakdown per serving:

Calories: 190 kcal, Protein: 6 grams, Carbohydrates: 26 grams, Fat: 7 grams, Saturated Fat: 1 grams, Cholesterol: 0 milligrams, Sodium: 35 milligrams, Fiber: 4 grams, and Sugar: 4 grams.

TOMATO AND MOZZARELLA SALAD WITH BASIL PESTO

Total Prep Time: 20 minutes
Total Cooking Time: 0 minutes
Servings: 4

Ingredients:

- 1 pound (450g) cherry or grape tomatoes, halved
- 8 ounces (225g) fresh mozzarella cheese, cut into 1/2-inch cubes
- 1/4 cup (40g) thinly sliced fresh basil leaves
- 2 tablespoons (30ml) olive oil
- 2 tablespoons (30ml) balsamic vinegar
- Salt and black pepper to taste

For the Basil Pesto:

- 2 cups (60g) fresh basil leaves
- 1/4 cup (40g) pine nuts or walnuts
- 2 cloves garlic, minced
- 1/4 cup (60ml) olive oil
- 2 tablespoons (30ml) freshly grated Parmesan cheese
- Salt and black pepper to taste

Instructions:

1. Combine basil, pine nuts or walnuts, and minced garlic in a food processor. Pulse until coarsely chopped. Create a smooth pesto by gradually adding olive oil to the processing mixture. Fold in Parmesan cheese and season generously with salt and pepper.
2. In a large bowl, combine the halved tomatoes, cubed mozzarella cheese, and thinly sliced fresh basil leaves.
3. Combine the tomato and mozzarella mixture with a drizzle of two tablespoons olive oil and two tablespoons balsamic vinegar. Toss gently.
4. Distribute the basil pesto evenly over the salad and delicately combine, taking care not to crumble the mozzarella.
5. Season the Tomato and Mozzarella Salad with Basil Pesto to your preference with salt and black pepper.

6. Enjoy the salad either cold or at ambient temperature.

Nutritional breakdown per serving:

Calories: 300 kcal, Protein: 13 grams, Carbohydrates: 10 grams, Fat: 25 grams, Saturated Fat: 7 grams, Cholesterol: 35 milligrams, Sodium: 340 milligrams, Fiber: 2 grams, and Sugar: 5 grams.

BAKED MEDITERRANEAN SALMON WITH ROASTED VEGGIES

Total Prep Time: 20 minutes
Total Cooking Time: 30 minutes
Servings: 4 (1 salmon fillet and 1 cup of veggies per serving)

Ingredients:

- 4 (6-ounce or 170g) salmon fillets
- 2 tablespoons (30ml) olive oil, plus extra
- 2 teaspoons (10ml) dried oregano
- 1 teaspoon (5ml) garlic powder
- 1 teaspoon (5ml) paprika
- Salt and black pepper to taste
- 1 red bell pepper, sliced
- 1 zucchini, halved lengthwise and sliced
- 1 red onion, sliced
- 2 cups (300g) cherry tomatoes, halved
- 2 tablespoons (30ml) lemon juice
- 2 tablespoons (10g) chopped fresh parsley

Instructions:

1. Get started by setting your oven temperature to 400°F (200°C).
2. Combine the olive oil, dried oregano, garlic powder, and paprika in a small bowl. Season to taste with salt and pepper.
3. Place the salmon fillets on a large, parchment-lined or silicone-matted baking sheet.
4. Coat the salmon fillets evenly with the seasoned olive oil mixture.
5. Combine sliced bell pepper, zucchini, red onion, and cherry tomatoes in a large bowl. Drizzle with olive oil and toss. Season the vegetables with salt and pepper.
6. Spread the seasoned vegetables around the salmon fillets on the baking sheet.
7. Roast the salmon and vegetables for 18-22 minutes, or until the salmon is cooked through and flaky and the vegetables are tender.
8. Take the baking sheet out of the oven and squeeze lemon juice over the salmon and vegetables.
9. Garnish with chopped fresh parsley.
10. Serve the Baked Mediterranean Salmon with the roasted vegetables immediately.

Nutritional breakdown per serving:

Calories: 340 kcal, Protein: 35 grams, Carbohydrates: 12 grams, Fat: 18 grams, Saturated Fat: 3 grams, Cholesterol: 80 milligrams, Sodium: 280 milligrams, Fiber: 3 grams, and Sugar: 5 grams.

LAMB AND EGGPLANT MOUSSAKA

Total Prep Time: 45 minutes
Total Cooking Time: 1 hour 15 minutes
Servings: 6

Ingredients:

- 2 medium eggplants, sliced into 1/2-inch thick rounds
- 3 tablespoons (45ml) olive oil, divided
- 1 pound (450g) ground lamb
- 1 onion, diced
- 3 cloves garlic, minced
- 1 teaspoon (5ml) ground cinnamon
- 1 teaspoon (5ml) dried oregano
- 1/2 teaspoon (2.5ml) ground allspice
- 1 (14.5-ounce or 410g) can diced tomatoes
- 2 tablespoons (30ml) tomato paste
- Salt and black pepper to taste

For the Béchamel Sauce:

- 4 tablespoons (60g) unsalted butter
- 1/4 cup (35g) all-purpose flour
- 2 cups (480ml) milk
- 1/4 teaspoon (1.25ml) ground nutmeg
- Salt and black pepper to taste
- 1/2 cup (50g) grated Parmesan cheese

Instructions:

1. Get started by setting your oven temperature to 400°F (200°C).
2. Spread the eggplant slices across two baking sheets. Coat the eggplant slices with 2 tablespoons of olive oil. Roast the eggplant for 15-20 minutes, or until tender and golden brown. Let cool.
3. Warm the leftover olive oil in a large skillet set over high heat. Add the ground lamb and brown, breaking it up with a spoon, for about 5 minutes.
4. To the heated skillet, add the diced onion and minced garlic. Sauté the ingredients for 2-3 minutes, or until the onion turns translucent.

5. Stir in the ground cinnamon, dried oregano, and ground allspice. Toast the spices by cooking them for 1 minute.
6. Combine the diced tomatoes and tomato paste with the other ingredients. Simmer until the sauce is thick, about 10-15 minutes. Finish by seasoning the mixture with salt and black pepper to your desired taste.
7. Melt butter over medium heat. Whisk in flour, cook 2 minutes. Gradually whisk in milk and cook, stirring continuously, until thickened (about 5-7 minutes). Season with nutmeg, salt, and pepper.
8. Grease a 9x13-inch baking dish. Arrange half the roasted eggplant slices at the bottom of the dish. Top with the lamb mixture, then the remaining eggplant slices.
9. Pour béchamel sauce over the dish. Sprinkle with Parmesan cheese.
10. Bake for 45-50 minutes, or until the top is golden brown and deeply browned.
11. Permit the moussaka to sit for 10-15 minutes prior to serving.

Nutritional breakdown per serving:

Calories: 450 kcal, Protein: 27 grams, Carbohydrates: 25 grams, Fat: 29 grams, Saturated Fat: 13 grams, Cholesterol: 85 milligrams, Sodium: 49 milligrams, Fiber: 6 grams, and Sugar: 10 grams.

MEDITERRANEAN CHICKEN AND ORZO SKILLET

Total Prep Time: 20 minutes
Total Cooking Time: 30 minutes
Servings: 4

Ingredients:

- 1 lb (450g) boneless, skinless chicken, cubed
- 2 tablespoons (30ml) olive oil
- 1 cup (185g) uncooked orzo pasta
- 1 cup (240ml) chicken broth
- 1 (14.5-ounce or 410g) can diced tomatoes
- 1 cup (150g) halved cherry tomatoes
- 1 cup (150g) pitted kalamata olives, halved
- 1/2 cup (75g) crumbled feta cheese
- 2 tablespoons (30ml) fresh lemon juice
- 1 teaspoon (5ml) dried oregano
- Salt and black pepper to taste
- 2 tablespoons (10g) chopped fresh parsley, for garnish

Instructions:

1. Warm a large skillet over medium-high heat. Add olive oil.
2. Transfer the cubed chicken to the preheated skillet and cook, stirring intermittently, until the chicken is lightly browned on all sides, around 5-7 minutes.
3. Add the uncooked orzo pasta to the skillet and mix it in to coat the pasta with the oil. Cook the orzo for 2-3 minutes, stirring frequently, until it's lightly toasted.
4. Add the chicken broth and diced tomatoes (including their juice) to the skillet. Allow the mixture to come to a light simmer, then decrease the heat to medium-low, cover the skillet, and cook for 10-12 minutes until the orzo is tender and has absorbed the majority of the liquid.
5. Stir in the halved cherry tomatoes, kalamata olives, crumbled feta cheese, lemon juice, and dried oregano. Customize the seasoning by adding salt and black pepper to the dish, adjusting the quantities to your liking.
6. Cook for an additional 2-3 minutes, or until the tomatoes are slightly softened and the flavors are combined.
7. Take the skillet off the heat, then top the Mediterranean Chicken and Orzo Skillet with the chopped fresh parsley as a garnish.

8. Serve the dish immediately.

Nutritional breakdown per serving:

Calories: 400 kcal, Protein: 30 grams, Carbohydrates: 34 grams, Fat: 16 grams, Saturated Fat: 4 grams, Cholesterol: 70 milligrams, Sodium: 820 milligrams, Fiber: 4 grams, and Sugar: 6 grams.

STUFFED PORTOBELLO MUSHROOMS WITH FETA AND SPINACH

Total Prep Time: 15 minutes
Total Cooking Time: 25 minutes
Servings: 4 (2 stuffed mushrooms per serving)

Ingredients:

- 8 large portobello mushrooms, stems removed and chopped
- 2 tablespoons (30ml) olive oil, divided
- 1 small onion, diced
- 3 cloves garlic, minced
- 5 ounces (140g) fresh spinach, chopped
- 1/2 cup (50g) crumbled feta cheese
- 2 tablespoons (10g) grated Parmesan cheese
- 1 teaspoon (5ml) dried oregano
- Salt and black pepper to taste

Instructions:

1. Get started by setting your oven temperature to 400°F (200°C).
2. Gently pat the portobello mushroom caps with a damp paper towel to clean them. Remove and chop the stems.
3. Set a large skillet over medium heat, then pour in 1 tablespoon of olive oil. Into the heated skillet, add the chopped mushroom stems, diced onion, and minced garlic. Sauté for 4-5 minutes, or until the onion is translucent.
4. Toss the chopped spinach into the skillet and cook for 2-3 more minutes, allowing the spinach to wilt. Remove the skillet from the heat and let the mixture cool slightly.
5. In a mixing bowl, mix together the sautéed mushroom stem and spinach mixture, crumbled feta cheese, grated Parmesan cheese, and dried oregano. Evaluate the seasoning of the mixture, then add salt and black pepper as needed, tailoring the amounts to your personal preferences.
6. Arrange the portobello mushroom caps, gill-side up, on a baking sheet. Brush the tops and sides of the mushroom caps with the remaining 1 tablespoon of olive oil.
7. Scoop the feta and spinach filling evenly into the mushroom caps, pressing down lightly to compact it.

8. Carefully position the stuffed portobello mushrooms in the preheated oven, allowing them to bake for 20-25 minutes until the mushrooms are soft and the filling is piping hot.
9. Serve the Stuffed Portobello Mushrooms with Feta and Spinach immediately.

Nutritional breakdown per serving:

Calories: 170 kcal, Protein: 10 grams, Carbohydrates: 10 grams, Fat: 12 grams, Saturated Fat: 4 grams, Cholesterol: 20 milligrams, Sodium: 390 milligrams, Fiber: 3 grams, and Sugar: 4 grams.

MEDITERRANEAN VEGETABLE AND QUINOA STUFFED PEPPERS

Total Prep Time: 20 minutes
Total Cooking Time: 40 minutes
Servings: 6 (1 stuffed pepper per serving)

Ingredients:

- 6 medium bell peppers (any color)
- 1 cup (185g) dry quinoa, rinsed
- 1 cup (240ml) vegetable or chicken broth
- 1 tablespoon (15ml) olive oil
- 1 medium onion, diced
- 3 cloves garlic, minced
- 1 (14.5-ounce or 410g) can diced tomatoes
- 1 cup (150g) halved cherry tomatoes
- 1/2 cup (75g) pitted kalamata olives, chopped
- 1/2 cup (75g) crumbled feta cheese
- 1/4 cup (10g) chopped fresh basil
- 1 teaspoon (5ml) dried oregano
- Salt and black pepper to taste

Instructions:

1. Get started by setting your oven temperature to 375°F (190°C).
2. First, slice off the tops of the bell peppers. Next, use a spoon to carefully remove and discard the seeds and inner white membranes from the peppers. Transfer the prepared bell peppers to a baking dish and set them aside.
3. Grab a medium-sized saucepan and add the rinsed quinoa and vegetable or chicken broth. Boil the quinoa and broth, then simmer covered for 15-18 minutes until the quinoa is tender and has absorbed the liquid. Fluff the prepared quinoa with a fork and set it aside.
4. Set a large skillet over medium heat and pour in the olive oil. Sauté the diced onion and minced garlic for 3-4 minutes, until the onion becomes translucent..
5. Add the diced tomatoes (with their juice), halved cherry tomatoes, chopped kalamata olives, crumbled feta cheese, chopped fresh basil, and dried oregano to the skillet. Season the prepared dish with salt and pepper to taste.

6. Stir the sautéed vegetables and seasonings into the cooked quinoa until well combined.
7. Spoon the Mediterranean vegetable and quinoa filling evenly into the hollowed-out bell peppers, pressing it down gently to compact it.
8. Put the stuffed peppers in the baking dish and cover with foil.
9. Bake the stuffed peppers, covered, in the preheated oven for 30-35 minutes, until the peppers are tender and the filling is hot throughout.
10. Serve the Mediterranean Vegetable and Quinoa Stuffed Peppers warm.

Nutritional breakdown per serving:

Calories: 220 kcal, Protein: 9 grams, Carbohydrates: 28 grams, Fat: 9 grams, Saturated Fat: 3 grams, Cholesterol: 15 milligrams, Sodium: 540 milligrams, Fiber: 5 grams, and Sugar: 8 grams.

ROASTED LEMON-GARLIC POTATOES WITH OREGANO

Total Prep Time: 15 minutes
Total Cooking Time: 40 minutes
Servings: 4 (about 1 cup per serving)

Ingredients:

- 2 pounds (900g) Yukon Gold potatoes, peeled and cut into 1-inch (2.5cm) cubes
- 3 tablespoons (45ml) olive oil
- 4 cloves garlic, minced
- 2 tablespoons (30ml) freshly squeezed lemon juice
- 1 teaspoon (5ml) dried oregano
- 1 teaspoon (5ml) salt
- 1/2 teaspoon (2.5ml) black pepper
- 2 tablespoons (10g) freshly grated Parmesan cheese (optional)
- 2 tablespoons (10g) chopped fresh parsley (optional)

Instructions:

1. Get started by setting your oven temperature to 400°F (200°C).
2. In a large bowl, create a mixture of cubed potatoes, olive oil, minced garlic, lemon juice, dried oregano, salt, and black pepper. Gently toss the ingredients together until the potato cubes are thoroughly coated.
3. Create a single layer of seasoned potato cubes on a spacious baking sheet. Make sure the potatoes are not overcrowded, as this will prevent them from browning properly.
4. Roast the coated potato cubes in the preheated oven for 35-40 minutes, flipping them halfway, until tender and golden-brown.
5. Take the roasted potatoes out of the oven and transfer them to a serving bowl.
6. Optionally, top the roasted lemon-garlic potatoes with freshly grated Parmesan cheese and chopped fresh parsley. Toss gently to combine.
7. Serve the Roasted Lemon-Garlic Potatoes with Oregano warm.

Nutritional breakdown per serving:

Calories: 220 kcal, Protein: 4 grams, Carbohydrates: 32 grams, Fat: 8 grams, Saturated Fat: 1.5 grams, Cholesterol: 0 milligrams, Sodium: 510 milligrams, Fiber: 4 grams, and Sugar: 3 grams.

MEDITERRANEAN CAULIFLOWER RICE PILAF

Total Prep Time: 15 minutes
Total Cooking Time: 25 minutes
Servings: 4 (about 1 cup per serving)

Ingredients:

- 1 medium cauliflower, florets (4 cups/500g)
- 2 tablespoons (30ml) olive oil
- 1 small onion, diced
- 3 cloves garlic, minced
- 1 cup (150g) cherry tomatoes, halved
- 1/2 cup (75g) pitted kalamata olives, sliced
- 1/4 cup (40g) crumbled feta cheese
- 2 tablespoons (10g) chopped fresh parsley
- 1 tablespoon (15ml) freshly squeezed lemon juice
- 1 teaspoon (5ml) dried oregano
- 1/2 teaspoon (2.5ml) salt
- 1/4 teaspoon (1.25ml) black pepper

Instructions:

1. Process cauliflower florets in short bursts within a food processor to achieve a rice-like texture. This should yield approximately 4 cups of cauliflower "rice".
2. Set a large skillet over medium heat and pour in the olive oil. Sauté the diced onion and minced garlic for 3-4 minutes, until the onion becomes translucent.
3. Put the cauliflower "rice" into the skillet and cook for 5-7 minutes, stirring periodically, until the cauliflower is tender and has softened a bit.
4. Stir in the halved cherry tomatoes, sliced kalamata olives, crumbled feta cheese, chopped fresh parsley, lemon juice, dried oregano, salt, and black pepper.
5. Cook the Mediterranean Cauliflower Rice Pilaf for an additional 2-3 minutes, or until the flavors are well combined and the tomatoes are slightly softened.
6. Take the skillet off the heat and serve the Mediterranean Cauliflower Rice Pilaf warm.

Nutritional breakdown per serving:

Calories: 180 kcal, Protein: 6 grams, Carbohydrates: 14 grams, Fat: 12 grams, Saturated Fat: 3 grams, Cholesterol: 15 milligrams, Sodium: 580 milligrams, Fiber: 4 grams, and Sugar: 4 grams.

BAKED FETA AND TOMATO ORZO

Total Prep Time: 20 minutes
Total Cooking Time: 35 minutes
Servings: 4 (about 1 cup per serving)

Ingredients:

- 1 cup (200g) uncooked orzo pasta
- 1 pint (300g) cherry or grape tomatoes, halved
- 4 ounces (115g) block of feta cheese, cut into 1-inch cubes
- 3 tablespoons (45ml) olive oil
- 2 cloves garlic, minced
- 1 teaspoon (5ml) dried oregano
- 1/4 teaspoon (1.25ml) crushed red pepper flakes (optional)
- 1/4 teaspoon (1.25ml) salt
- 1/4 teaspoon (1.25ml) black pepper
- 2 tablespoons (10g) freshly grated Parmesan cheese
- 2 tablespoons (10g) chopped fresh basil

Instructions:

1. Get started by setting your oven temperature to 400°F (200°C).
2. Prepare the orzo as instructed on the package. Drain off any excess water.
3. In a large baking dish, arrange the halved cherry or grape tomatoes and cubes of feta cheese.
4. To make the dressing, whisk olive oil, minced garlic, dried oregano, a dash of red pepper flakes (optional), salt, and black pepper in a small bowl.
5. Drizzle the garlic-herb oil over the tomatoes and feta in the baking dish, and gently toss to combine.
6. Bake the tomato and feta mixture in a preheated oven for 20-25 minutes, or until the tomatoes have softened and the feta is lightly browned.
7. Take the baking dish out of the oven and gently fold in the cooked orzo, ensuring the pasta is thoroughly coated in the tomato-feta juices.
8. Sprinkle the Parmesan cheese and chopped fresh basil over the top of the Baked Feta and Tomato Orzo.
9. Serve the dish warm.

Nutritional breakdown per serving:

Calories: 320 kcal, Protein: 10 grams, Carbohydrates: 33 grams, Fat: 16 grams, Saturated Fat: 5 grams, Cholesterol: 25 milligrams, Sodium: 460 milligrams, Fiber: 3 grams, and Sugar: 7 grams.

MEDITERRANEAN ROASTED VEGETABLE MEDLEY

Total Prep Time: 20 minutes
Total Cooking Time: 40 minutes
Servings: 6 (about 1 cup per serving)

Ingredients:

- 1 medium eggplant, cut into 1-inch cubes (about 2 cups or 300g)
- 1 medium zucchini, diced into 1-inch pieces (approximately 2 cups or 300g)
- 1 red bell pepper, diced
- 1 yellow onion, cut into 1-inch pieces (about 1 cup or 150g)
- 3 cloves garlic, minced
- 2 tablespoons (30ml) olive oil
- 1 teaspoon (5ml) dried oregano
- 1 teaspoon (5ml) dried basil
- 1/2 teaspoon (2.5ml) salt
- 1/4 teaspoon (1.25ml) black pepper
- 1/4 cup (40g) kalamata olives, halved
- 2 tablespoons (10g) chopped fresh parsley
- 2 tablespoons (10g) crumbled feta cheese (optional)

Instructions:

1. Get started by setting your oven temperature to 400°F (200°C).
2. Combine all the chopped vegetables (eggplant, zucchini, bell pepper, and onion) in a large bowl.
3. Infuse the vegetables with flavor by adding minced garlic, olive oil, dried oregano, basil, salt, and pepper. Toss well to coat.
4. Create a single layer of seasoned vegetables on a large baking sheet.
5. Roast the vegetables for 35-40 minutes in a preheated oven, stirring them midway through cooking. They are done when tender and lightly browned.
6. Take the roasted vegetables out of the oven and place them in a serving bowl.
7. Gently stir in the halved kalamata olives and chopped fresh parsley.
8. If desired, sprinkle the Mediterranean Roasted Vegetable Medley with crumbled feta cheese.
9. Serve the dish either hot or chilled.

Nutritional breakdown per serving:

Calories: 120 kcal, Protein: 3 grams, Carbohydrates: 14 grams, Fat: 6 grams, Saturated Fat: 1 grams, Cholesterol: 0 milligrams, Sodium: 320 milligrams, Fiber: 4 grams, and Sugar: 4 grams.

HERBED CHICKPEA AND ARTICHOKE DIP WITH PITA CHIPS

Total Prep Time: 20 minutes
Total Cooking Time: 15 minutes
Servings: 8 (about 1/4 cup of dip per serving)

Ingredients:

Dip:

- 1 (15 oz or 425g) can of chickpeas (garbanzo beans), rinsed and drained
- 1 (14 oz or 400g) can of artichoke hearts, drained and chopped
- 3 tablespoons (45ml) olive oil
- 2 tablespoons (30ml) freshly squeezed lemon juice
- 2 cloves garlic, minced
- 2 tablespoons (10g) chopped fresh parsley
- 1 tablespoon (5g) chopped fresh oregano
- 1/2 teaspoon (2.5ml) salt
- 1/4 teaspoon (1.25ml) black pepper

Pita Chips:

- 4 (6-inch) pita breads, cut into 8 triangles each
- 2 tablespoons (30ml) olive oil
- 1/2 teaspoon (2.5ml) garlic powder
- 1/4 teaspoon (1.25ml) salt

Instructions:

Pita Chips:

1. Get started by setting your oven temperature to 400°F (200°C).
2. In a spacious bowl, mix the pita bread triangles with olive oil, garlic powder, and salt until evenly seasoned.
3. Position the pita chips in a flat layer on a spacious baking sheet.
4. Bake the pita chips in the preheated oven for 10-12 minutes, or until they are golden brown and crispy. Set aside.

Dip:

1. Add rinsed and drained chickpeas, chopped artichoke hearts, olive oil, lemon juice, minced garlic, parsley, oregano, salt, and pepper to a food processor. Process until smooth or chunky, as preferred.
2. Process the mixture in pulses until it has a slightly chunky texture. Pause to scrape down the sides of the food processor as necessary.
3. Transfer the Herbed Chickpea and Artichoke Dip to a serving bowl.
4. Serve the dip immediately with the baked pita chips.

Nutritional breakdown per serving:

Calories: 200 kcal, Protein: 3 grams, Carbohydrates: 22 grams, Fat: 11 grams, Saturated Fat: 1 grams, Cholesterol: 0 milligrams, Sodium: 530 milligrams, Fiber: 5 grams, and Sugar: 5 grams.

ROASTED GARLIC AND LEMON BROCCOLI

Total Prep Time: 10 minutes
Total Cooking Time: 20 minutes
Servings: 4 (about 1 cup per serving)

Ingredients:

- 1 lb (454g) broccoli florets, cut into bite-sized pieces
- 3 tablespoons (45ml) olive oil
- 3 cloves garlic, minced
- 1 tablespoon (15ml) freshly squeezed lemon juice
- 1/2 teaspoon (2.5ml) grated lemon zest
- 1/2 teaspoon (2.5ml) salt
- 1/4 teaspoon (1.25ml) black pepper
- 2 tablespoons (10g) grated Parmesan cheese (optional)
- 2 tablespoons (10g) chopped fresh parsley (optional)

Instructions:

1. Get started by setting your oven temperature to 400°F (200°C).
2. Toss broccoli florets with a mixture of olive oil, minced garlic, lemon juice, lemon zest, salt, and pepper in a large bowl until thoroughly coated.
3. Create a single layer of seasoned broccoli on a spacious baking sheet.
4. Place the broccoli in the preheated oven and roast for 15-20 minutes, or until tender and golden. Toss the broccoli midway through the cooking process.
5. Take the roasted broccoli out of the oven and place it in a serving bowl.
6. If desired, sprinkle the Roasted Garlic and Lemon Broccoli with grated Parmesan cheese and chopped fresh parsley.
7. Serve the broccoli warm.

Nutritional breakdown per serving:

Calories: 120 kcal, Protein: 4 grams, Carbohydrates: 8 grams, Fat: 9 grams, Saturated Fat: 1.5 grams, Cholesterol: 0 milligrams, Sodium: 350 milligrams, Fiber: 3 grams, and Sugar: 3 grams.

MEDITERRANEAN QUINOA TABBOULEH

Total Prep Time: 15 minutes
Total Cooking Time: 20 minutes
Servings: 6 (about 1 cup per serving)

Ingredients:

- 1 cup (185g) uncooked quinoa, rinsed
- 1 1/2 cups (355ml) vegetable broth or water
- 1 cup (150g) diced cucumber
- 1 cup (150g) diced tomatoes
- 1/2 cup (75g) diced red onion
- 1/2 cup (20g) chopped fresh parsley
- 1/4 cup (10g) chopped fresh mint
- 3 tablespoons (45ml) freshly squeezed lemon juice
- 2 tablespoons (30ml) olive oil
- 1 teaspoon (5ml) ground cumin
- 1/2 teaspoon (2.5ml) salt
- 1/4 teaspoon (1.25ml) black pepper

Instructions:

1. In a medium saucepan, unite the rinsed quinoa and vegetable broth (or water). Bring to a boil over high heat.
2. Simmer the quinoa, covered, for 15-20 minutes after boiling, until it's fully cooked and the liquid has been absorbed.
3. Remove the saucepan from the heat and let the quinoa cool to room temperature.
4. Combine the cooked and cooled quinoa, diced cucumber, diced tomatoes, diced red onion, chopped parsley, and chopped mint in a large bowl.
5. Whisk together lemon juice, olive oil, cumin, salt, and pepper in a small bowl to form a dressing.
6. Pour the lemon-olive oil dressing over the quinoa mixture and toss gently to coat.
7. Serve the Mediterranean Quinoa Tabbouleh chilled or at room temperature.

Nutritional breakdown per serving:

Calories: 180 kcal, Protein: 6 grams, Carbohydrates: 24 grams, Fat: 8 grams, Saturated Fat: 1 grams, Cholesterol: 0 milligrams, Sodium: 300 milligrams, Fiber: 4 grams, and Sugar: 5 grams.

BAKED FETA AND SPINACH STUFFED TOMATOES

Total Prep Time: 20 minutes
Total Cooking Time: 25 minutes
Servings: 6 (1 stuffed tomato per serving)

Ingredients:

- 6 medium-sized tomatoes
- 2 cups (60g) fresh baby spinach, chopped
- 4 ounces (113g) crumbled feta cheese
- 2 tablespoons (30ml) olive oil, divided
- 2 cloves garlic, minced
- 1/4 cup (10g) chopped fresh basil
- 1/4 teaspoon (1.25ml) red pepper flakes (optional)
- Salt and black pepper to taste

Instructions:

1. Get started by setting your oven temperature to 400°F (200°C).
2. Cut off the tops of the tomatoes and extract the pulp and seeds. Reserve the hollow tomato shells. Dice the removed tomato pulp.
3. Toss together chopped tomato pulp, spinach, crumbled feta, a tablespoon of olive oil, minced garlic, chopped basil, and red pepper flakes (optional) in a medium bowl. Season generously with salt and pepper.
4. Arrange the hollowed-out tomato shells in a baking dish or on a rimmed baking sheet.
5. Spoon the feta and spinach mixture evenly into the tomato shells.
6. Drizzle the remaining 1 tablespoon (15ml) of olive oil over the stuffed tomatoes.
7. Roast the stuffed tomatoes in a preheated oven for 20-25 minutes, or until the tomatoes are tender and the filling is heated through.
8. Serve the Baked Feta and Spinach Stuffed Tomatoes warm.

Nutritional breakdown per serving:

Calories: 120 kcal, Protein: 6 grams, Carbohydrates: 8 grams, Fat: 8 grams, Saturated Fat: 3 grams, Cholesterol: 15 milligrams, Sodium: 320 milligrams, Fiber: 2 grams, and Sugar: 6 grams.

ROASTED RED PEPPER AND WALNUT HUMMUS WITH PITA BREAD

Total Prep Time: 15 minutes
Total Cooking Time: 20 minutes
Servings: 8 (about 1/4 cup hummus per serving)

Ingredients:

Hummus:

- 1 (15 oz) can chickpeas, drained and rinsed
- 1/2 cup (75g) roasted red peppers, drained and chopped
- 1/3 cup (40g) toasted walnuts
- 2 tablespoons (30ml) tahini
- 2 tablespoons (30ml) freshly squeezed lemon juice
- 1 clove garlic, minced
- 2 tablespoons (30ml) olive oil
- 1/4 teaspoon (1.25ml) ground cumin
- 1/4 teaspoon (1.25ml) smoked paprika
- Salt and black pepper to taste

Pita Bread:

- 4 whole-wheat pita breads, cut into wedges

Instructions:

Hummus:

1. Get started by setting your oven temperature to 400°F (200°C).

2. Spread the walnuts on a baking sheet and toast them in the preheated oven for 5-7 minutes, or until fragrant and lightly browned. Allow the walnuts to cool slightly.

3. In a food processor, combine the drained and rinsed chickpeas, roasted red peppers, toasted walnuts, tahini, lemon juice, garlic, olive oil, cumin, and smoked paprika. Process the mixture until it is smooth and creamy, scraping down the sides as needed.

4. Season the hummus with salt and black pepper to taste.

Pita Bread:

    5. Cut the pita breads into wedges.

To Serve:

    6. Transfer the Roasted Red Pepper and Walnut Hummus to a serving bowl.

    7. Arrange the pita bread wedges around the hummus.

    8. Serve the hummus with the pita bread.

Nutritional breakdown per serving:

Calories: 160 kcal, Protein: 5 grams, Carbohydrates: 15 grams, Fat: 10 grams, Saturated Fat: 1 grams, Cholesterol: 0 milligrams, Sodium: 210 milligrams, Fiber: 4 grams, and Sugar: 4 grams.

GRILLED ZUCCHINI ROLLS WITH RICOTTA AND HERBS

Total Prep Time: 25 minutes
Total Cooking Time: 10 minutes
Servings: 8 (1 roll per serving)

Ingredients:

- 2 medium zucchini, sliced lengthwise, 1/4" thick
- 1 cup (240g) part-skim ricotta cheese
- 1/4 cup (10g) chopped fresh basil
- 2 tablespoons (8g) chopped fresh parsley
- 1 tablespoon (15ml) lemon juice
- 1 clove garlic, minced
- 1/4 teaspoon (1.25ml) salt
- 1/8 teaspoon (0.6ml) black pepper

Instructions:

1. Preheat your grill or grill pan.
2. Lightly oil both sides of the zucchini slices.
3. Grill the zucchini slices for 2-3 minutes per side, or until they are tender and have grill marks. Take the item off the grill and let it rest for a short time to cool down.
4. In a small bowl, blend ricotta cheese with chopped basil, parsley, lemon juice, minced garlic, salt, and pepper until smooth.
5. Lay the grilled zucchini slices on a flat surface. Place approximately 2 tablespoons of the ricotta mixture in the middle of each zucchini slice.
6. Carefully roll up the zucchini slices around the ricotta mixture, starting from the short end.
7. Arrange the Grilled Zucchini Rolls seam-side down on a serving platter.
8. Serve the Grilled Zucchini Rolls immediately, or chill in the refrigerator until ready to serve.

Nutritional breakdown per serving:

Calories: 60 kcal, Protein: 5 grams, Carbohydrates: 5 grams, Fat: 3 grams, Saturated Fat: 1 grams, Cholesterol: 5 milligrams, Sodium: 150 milligrams, Fiber: 1 grams, and Sugar: 5 grams.

MEDITERRANEAN BULGUR WHEAT SALAD WITH CUCUMBER AND FETA

Total Prep Time: 20 minutes
Total Cooking Time: 15 minutes
Servings: 6 (about 1 cup per serving)

Ingredients:

- 1 cup (185g) uncooked bulgur wheat
- 1 1/2 cups (355ml) low-sodium vegetable or chicken broth
- 1 cucumber, diced
- 1 cup (150g) crumbled feta cheese
- 1/2 cup (80g) halved cherry tomatoes
- 1/4 cup (10g) chopped fresh parsley
- 2 tablespoons (30ml) lemon juice
- 2 tablespoons (30ml) olive oil
- 1 clove garlic, minced
- 1/2 teaspoon (2.5ml) dried oregano
- 1/4 teaspoon (1.25ml) salt
- 1/4 teaspoon (1.25ml) black pepper

Instructions:

1. Boil broth in medium pan. Add the uncooked bulgur wheat, cover, and remove from heat. Let the bulgur wheat sit for 15 minutes, or until it has absorbed all the liquid. Lightly separate the mixture with a fork and allow it to cool slightly.
2. Combine cooked, cooled bulgur wheat, diced cucumber, crumbled feta, halved cherry tomatoes, and chopped parsley in a large bowl.
3. Combine lemon juice, olive oil, garlic, oregano, salt, and pepper in a small bowl. Whisk until blended.
4. Pour the lemon-garlic dressing over the bulgur wheat salad and toss gently to coat.
5. Serve the Mediterranean Bulgur Wheat Salad chilled or at room temperature.

Nutritional breakdown per serving:

Calories: 220 kcal, Protein: 8 grams, Carbohydrates: 23 grams, Fat: 11 grams, Saturated Fat: 4 grams, Cholesterol: 20 milligrams, Sodium: 450 milligrams, Fiber: 5 grams, and Sugar: 6 grams.

BAKED EGGPLANT PARMESAN STACKS

Total Prep Time: 30 minutes
Total Cooking Time: 45 minutes
Servings: 6 (1 stack per serving)

Ingredients:

- 2 medium eggplants, sliced into 1/2-inch thick rounds
- 1 cup (120g) panko breadcrumbs
- 1/2 cup (50g) grated Parmesan cheese
- 1 teaspoon (5ml) Italian seasoning
- 1/2 teaspoon (2.5ml) garlic powder
- 1/4 teaspoon (1.25ml) salt
- 1/4 teaspoon (1.25ml) black pepper
- 1 egg, beaten
- 1 1/2 cups (355ml) marinara sauce
- 1 cup (120g) shredded mozzarella cheese

Instructions:

1. Get started by setting your oven temperature to 375°F (190°C). Cover baking sheet with parchment or silicone mat.
2. Combine panko, Parmesan, Italian seasoning, garlic powder, salt, and pepper in a shallow bowl. Stir to mix.
3. Coat eggplant slices in beaten egg, then in breadcrumb mixture. Press gently to adhere.
4. Place breaded eggplant slices in a single layer on baking sheet.
5. Bake the eggplant slices for 20-25 minutes, flipping them halfway through, until they are golden brown and tender.
6. Take baked eggplant from oven. Top each slice with marinara sauce and mozzarella cheese.
7. Create six stacks of eggplant slices. Place stacks back in oven and bake 10-15 minutes more, or until cheese is melted and bubbly.
8. Serve eggplant stacks hot, optionally garnished with fresh basil or parsley.

Nutritional breakdown per serving:

Calories: 240 kcal, Protein: 13 grams, Carbohydrates: 29 grams, Fat: 9 grams, Saturated Fat: 4 grams, Cholesterol: 50 milligrams, Sodium: 700 milligrams, Fiber: 7 grams, and Sugar: 8 grams.

MEDITERRANEAN LENTIL AND SWEET POTATO PATTIES

Total Prep Time: 30 minutes
Total Cooking Time: 20 minutes
Servings: 8 (1 patty per serving)

Ingredients:

- 1 cup (200g) cooked brown or green lentils, drained and rinsed
- 1 medium grated peeled sweet potato (about 1 cup)
- 1/2 cup (60g) whole wheat breadcrumbs
- 2 tablespoons (10g) chopped fresh parsley
- 2 tablespoons (10g) chopped fresh basil
- 1 clove garlic, minced
- 1 teaspoon (5ml) ground cumin
- 1/2 teaspoon (2.5ml) paprika
- 1/4 teaspoon (1.25ml) salt
- 1/4 teaspoon (1.25ml) black pepper
- 1 tablespoon (15ml) olive oil

Instructions:

1. In a large bowl, mix together the cooked lentils, grated sweet potato, whole wheat breadcrumbs, chopped parsley, chopped basil, minced garlic, ground cumin, paprika, salt, and black pepper until well combined.
2. Using your hands, form the mixture into 8 equal-sized patties, about 1/2 inch thick.
3. Drizzle olive oil into a large non-stick skillet and place it over medium heat.
4. Working in batches if necessary, cook the lentil and sweet potato patties for 3-4 minutes per side, or until golden brown and crispy.
5. Drain the cooked patties on a paper towel-lined plate.
6. Serve the Mediterranean Lentil and Sweet Potato Patties warm, with your favorite toppings or sauces, such as tzatziki, hummus, or a fresh salad.

Nutritional breakdown per serving:

Calories: 110 kcal, Protein: 5 grams, Carbohydrates: 16 grams, Fat: 0 grams, Saturated Fat: 0.5 grams, Cholesterol: 0 milligrams, Sodium: 160 milligrams, Fiber: 4 grams, and Sugar: 6 grams.

ROASTED GARLIC AND HERB OLIVE OIL BREAD DIP

Total Prep Time: 15 minutes
Total Cooking Time: 35 minutes
Servings: 8 (2 tablespoons per serving)

Ingredients:

- 1 head of garlic
- 2 tablespoon (30ml) olive oil, extra
- 1/4 cup (60ml) extra-virgin olive oil
- 1 tablespoon (15ml) lemon juice
- 1 tablespoon (2g) chopped fresh basil
- 1 tablespoon (2g) chopped fresh parsley
- 1 teaspoon (5ml) dried oregano
- 1/4 teaspoon (1.25ml) red pepper flakes (optional)
- 1/4 teaspoon (1.25ml) salt
- 1/4 teaspoon (1.25ml) black pepper
- Crusty bread, for serving

Instructions:

1. Get started by setting your oven temperature to 400°F (200°C).
2. Cut the top off the head of garlic to expose the cloves. Arrange the garlic on a small piece of aluminum foil, pour 2 tablespoons of olive oil over it, then wrap the foil around the garlic to create a sealed packet.
3. Roast the garlic packet in the preheated oven for 30-35 minutes, or until the cloves are very soft and have turned golden in color. Once the oven time is up, take the garlic packet out and let it cool down for a short while.
4. Carefully extract the roasted garlic cloves from their skins and transfer them to a medium-sized bowl.
5. In the bowl containing the roasted garlic cloves, mix in 1/4 cup of extra-virgin olive oil, lemon juice, chopped basil, chopped parsley, dried oregano, red pepper flakes (if using), salt, and black pepper. Mash and stir the ingredients together until well combined.
6. Transfer the roasted garlic and herb olive oil dip to a serving bowl. Finish by drizzling a small amount of additional olive oil over the top.

7. Serve the Roasted Garlic and Herb Olive Oil Bread Dip with crusty bread for dipping.

Nutritional breakdown per serving:

Calories: 120 kcal, Protein: 0 grams, Carbohydrates: 1 grams, Fat: 13 grams, Saturated Fat: 2 grams, Cholesterol: 0 milligrams, Sodium: 100 milligrams, Fiber: 0 grams, and Sugar: 0 grams.

MEDITERRANEAN VEGETABLE COUSCOUS SALAD

Total Prep Time: 20 minutes
Total Cooking Time: 15 minutes
Servings: 6 (about 1 cup per serving)

Ingredients:

- 1 cup (175g) uncooked couscous
- 1 cup (240ml) boiling water
- 1 medium zucchini, diced
- 1 medium bell pepper, diced
- 1 cup (150g) cherry tomatoes, halved
- 1/2 cup (80g) diced cucumber
- 1/4 cup (10g) chopped fresh parsley
- 2 tablespoons (30ml) lemon juice
- 2 tablespoons (30ml) olive oil
- 1 clove garlic, minced
- 1 teaspoon (5ml) dried oregano
- 1/4 teaspoon (1.25ml) salt
- 1/4 teaspoon (1.25ml) black pepper

Instructions:

1. In a medium bowl, combine the uncooked couscous and boiling water. Cover the bowl and let it sit for 5 minutes, or until the couscous has fully absorbed all the liquid.
2. Fluff the freshly cooked couscous with a fork and let it rest for a short while to cool down a bit.
3. In a large bowl, gather the diced zucchini, diced bell pepper, halved cherry tomatoes, diced cucumber, and chopped parsley, then combine them all together.
4. Add the cooked and cooled couscous to the vegetable mixture.
5. Combine lemon juice, olive oil, minced garlic, dried oregano, salt, and pepper in a bowl. Whisk until blended.
6. Drizzle dressing over couscous and vegetables. Toss gently to coat.
7. Serve the Mediterranean Vegetable Couscous Salad chilled or at room temperature.

Nutritional breakdown per serving:

Calories: 180 kcal, Protein: 5 grams, Carbohydrates: 26 grams, Fat: 7 grams, Saturated Fat: 1 grams, Cholesterol: 0 milligrams, Sodium: 210 milligrams, Fiber: 3 grams, and Sugar: 6 grams.

CHAPTER 3
DELICIOUS LUNCH AND DINNER IDEAS

BAKED MEDITERRANEAN COD WITH TOMATOES AND OLIVES

Total Prep Time: 15 minutes
Total Cooking Time: 20 minutes
Servings: 4 (1 cod fillet per serving)

Ingredients:

- 4 (6-ounce or 170g) cod fillets
- 1 tablespoon (15ml) olive oil
- 2 cloves garlic, minced
- 1 (14.5 oz or 411g) can diced tomatoes, with juices
- 1/2 cup (75g) pitted kalamata olives, sliced
- 2 tablespoons (10g) chopped fresh parsley
- 1 teaspoon (5ml) dried oregano
- 1/4 teaspoon (1.25ml) red pepper flakes (optional)
- Salt and black pepper to taste

Instructions:

1. Get started by setting your oven temperature to 400°F (200°C).
2. Dry cod fillets with paper towels. Season with salt and pepper.
3. Warm olive oil in a large oven-safe pan. Soften garlic until fragrant.
4. Add the diced tomatoes with their juices, sliced kalamata olives, chopped parsley, dried oregano, and red pepper flakes (if using). Stir to combine.
5. Nestle the seasoned cod fillets into the tomato-olive mixture, making sure they are evenly distributed.
6. Roast the skillet or baking dish in the preheated oven for 15-20 minutes, or until the cod flakes easily.
7. Serve the Baked Mediterranean Cod with Tomatoes and Olives immediately, spooning the tomato-olive sauce over the top of the fish.

Nutritional breakdown per serving:

Calories: 260 kcal, Protein: 29 grams, Carbohydrates: 9 grams, Fat: 12 grams, Saturated Fat: 2 grams, Cholesterol: 75 milligrams, Sodium: 760 milligrams, Fiber: 2 grams, and Sugar: 5 grams.

GRILLED SWORDFISH KEBABS WITH LEMON-HERB MARINADE

Total Prep Time: 20 minutes
Total Cooking Time: 12-15 minutes
Servings: 4 (2 skewers per serving)

Ingredients:

- 1 lb (454g) swordfish, cut into 1-inch cubes
- 1 medium zucchini, cut into 1-inch cubes
- 1 red bell pepper, 1-inch pieces
- 1 red onion, cut into 1-inch pieces
- Marinade:
- 1/4 cup (60ml) olive oil
- 2 tablespoons (30ml) lemon juice
- 2 tablespoons (10g) chopped fresh parsley
- 1 tablespoon (5g) chopped fresh oregano
- 2 cloves garlic, minced
- 1 teaspoon (5ml) grated lemon zest
- 1/2 teaspoon (2.5ml) salt
- 1/4 teaspoon (1.25ml) black pepper

Instructions:

1. Combine olive oil, lemon juice, chopped parsley, oregano, minced garlic, lemon zest, salt, and black pepper in a medium bowl. Whisk until thoroughly blended.
2. Add the cubed swordfish, zucchini, bell pepper, and onion to the marinade. Toss to coat evenly. Cover and refrigerate for 15-30 minutes.
3. Preheat your grill to medium-high heat.
4. Thread the marinated swordfish and vegetables onto metal or wooden skewers, alternating the ingredients.
5. Allow the kebabs to grill for 12 to 15 minutes, flipping them over occasionally. Cook until the swordfish is fully cooked and easily flakes when pierced with a fork.
6. Serve the Grilled Swordfish Kebabs with Lemon-Herb Marinade immediately.

Nutritional breakdown per serving:

Calories: 280 kcal, Protein: 32 grams, Carbohydrates: 10 grams, Fat: 13 grams, Saturated Fat: 2 grams, Cholesterol: 80 milligrams, Sodium: 420 milligrams, Fiber: 2 grams, and Sugar: 5 grams.

MEDITERRANEAN SHRIMP SCAMPI WITH ZUCCHINI NOODLES

Total Prep Time: 20 minutes
Total Cooking Time: 15 minutes
Servings: 4 (about 1 1/2 cups per serving)

Ingredients:

- 3 medium zucchini, spiralized or julienned to make zucchini noodles
- 1 lb (454g) large shrimp, peeled and deveined
- 3 tablespoons (45ml) olive oil
- 4 cloves garlic, minced
- 1/4 cup (60ml) dry white wine
- 2 tablespoons (30ml) lemon juice
- 2 tablespoons (10g) chopped fresh parsley
- 1 teaspoon (5ml) lemon zest
- 1/4 teaspoon (1.25ml) red pepper flakes (optional)
- Salt and black pepper to taste

Instructions:

1. In a large skillet, add olive oil. Heat over medium heat. When hot, add minced garlic and cook until fragrant, about 60 seconds.
2. Place the shrimp in the pan and cook until they change color to pink and curl, approximately 2-3 minutes.
3. Introduce white wine and lemon juice to the pan. Let the mixture gently simmer for 2-3 minutes, or until the shrimp are fully cooked.
4. Add the zucchini noodles and mix carefully to distribute evenly. Continue cooking for 2-3 minutes more, or until the zucchini noodles soften.
5. Turn off the heat. Fold in chopped parsley, lemon zest, and red pepper flakes (if desired). Season generously with salt and pepper.
6. Serve the Mediterranean Shrimp Scampi with Zucchini Noodles immediately.

Nutritional breakdown per serving:

Calories: 240 kcal, Protein: 23 grams, Carbohydrates: 10 grams, Fat: 13 grams, Saturated Fat: 2 grams, Cholesterol: 220 milligrams, Sodium: 530 milligrams, Fiber: 2 grams, and Sugar: 5 grams.

BAKED STUFFED CALAMARI WITH SPINACH AND FETA

Total Prep Time: 30 minutes
Total Cooking Time: 30 minutes
Servings: 4 (2-3 stuffed calamari per serving)

Ingredients:

- 1 lb (454g) whole calamari, bodies cleaned and tentacles reserved
- 2 tablespoons (30ml) olive oil
- 1/2 cup (75g) diced onion
- 2 cloves garlic, minced
- 4 cups (120g) fresh spinach, chopped
- 1/2 cup (100g) crumbled feta cheese
- 1/4 cup (40g) panko breadcrumbs
- 2 tablespoons (10g) chopped fresh parsley
- 1 tablespoon (15ml) lemon juice
- 1/4 teaspoon (1.25ml) red pepper flakes (optional)
- Salt and black pepper to taste

Instructions:

1. Get started by setting your oven temperature to 400°F (200°C).
2. Heat a large skillet over medium heat. Add olive oil. Add diced onion and minced garlic. Cook for 2-3 minutes, or until the onion loses its raw appearance.
3. Combine the chopped spinach with the pan contents and cook until wilted, approximately 2-3 minutes. Remove from heat and let cool somewhat.
4. In a mixing bowl, blend together cooked spinach, crumbled feta, panko breadcrumbs, chopped parsley, lemon juice, and red pepper flakes (if using). Adjust the seasoning with salt and pepper.
5. Carefully stuff the spinach-feta mixture into the cleaned calamari bodies, being careful not to overstuff.
6. Arrange the stuffed calamari in a baking dish or on a rimmed baking sheet.
7. Bake the stuffed calamari for 25-30 minutes, or until the calamari is cooked through and the filling is hot and bubbly.
8. Serve the Baked Stuffed Calamari with Spinach and Feta immediately, garnished with the reserved calamari tentacles (if desired).

Nutritional breakdown per serving:

Calories: 220 kcal, Protein: 20 grams, Carbohydrates: 12 grams, Fat: 10 grams, Saturated Fat: 4 grams, Cholesterol: 320 milligrams, Sodium: 630 milligrams, Fiber: 2 grams, and Sugar: 5 grams.

MEDITERRANEAN TUNA STUFFED AVOCADOS

Total Prep Time: 15 minutes
Total Cooking Time: 0 minutes
Servings: 4 (1 stuffed avocado half per serving)

Ingredients:

- 2 large ripe avocados, halved and pits removed
- 1 (5 oz / 142g) can of tuna, drained
- 2 tablespoons (30ml) olive oil
- 1 tablespoon (15ml) lemon juice
- 2 tablespoons (10g) chopped fresh parsley
- 2 tablespoons (10g) chopped fresh basil
- 2 tablespoons (20g) crumbled feta cheese
- 1 tablespoon (15ml) capers, drained
- 1/4 teaspoon (1.25ml) red pepper flakes (optional)
- Salt and black pepper to taste

Instructions:

1. Cut the avocados in half lengthwise and remove the seeds. Carefully remove a small amount of avocado flesh from the center of each avocado half, forming a hollow space for the tuna mixture.
2. In a medium bowl, whisk together drained tuna, olive oil, lemon juice, chopped parsley and basil, crumbled feta, capers, and red pepper flakes (if desired). Adjust seasoning with salt and pepper.
3. Spoon the tuna mixture evenly into the hollowed-out avocado halves.
4. Arrange the stuffed avocado halves on a serving plate or platter.
5. Serve the Mediterranean Tuna Stuffed Avocados immediately.

Nutritional breakdown per serving:

Calories: 260 kcal, Protein: 15 grams, Carbohydrates: 12 grams, Fat: 19 grams, Saturated Fat: 4 grams, Cholesterol: 35 milligrams, Sodium: 440 milligrams, Fiber: 7 grams, and Sugar: 5 grams.

GRILLED SALMON SKEWERS WITH MEDITERRANEAN SALSA

Total Prep Time: 30 minutes
Total Cooking Time: 12-15 minutes
Servings: 4 (2-3 skewers per serving)

Ingredients:

Salmon Skewers:

- 1 lb (454g) salmon fillets, cut into 1-inch cubes
- 2 tablespoons (30ml) olive oil
- 1 tablespoon (15ml) lemon juice
- 2 cloves garlic, minced
- 1 teaspoon (5ml) dried oregano
- Salt and black pepper to taste

Mediterranean Salsa:

- 1 cup (150g) diced tomatoes
- 1/2 cup (75g) diced cucumber
- 1/4 cup (40g) diced red onion
- 2 tablespoons (10g) chopped fresh parsley
- 2 tablespoons (10g) chopped fresh basil
- 1 tablespoon (15ml) lemon juice
- 1 tablespoon (15ml) olive oil
- 1 clove garlic, minced
- 1/4 teaspoon (1.25ml) red pepper flakes (optional)
- Salt and black pepper to taste

Instructions:

1. Combine diced salmon with olive oil, lemon juice, minced garlic, and dried oregano in a bowl. Season salmon with salt and pepper. Toss.
2. To prevent wooden skewers from burning, submerge them in water for 30 minutes before grilling. Thread the salmon cubes onto the skewers.

3. In a mixing bowl, unite diced tomatoes, cucumber, red onion, chopped parsley and basil. Season with lemon juice, olive oil, minced garlic, and a touch of red pepper flakes if you prefer. Season generously with salt and black pepper.
4. Stir the salsa ingredients together until well combined.
5. Allow your grill or grill pan to reach a medium-high temperature before starting.
6. Grill the salmon skewers for 12-15 minutes, turning occasionally, until the salmon is cooked through and flakes easily with a fork.
7. Serve the grilled salmon skewers immediately, topped with the Mediterranean salsa.

Nutritional breakdown per serving:

Calories: 300 kcal, Protein: 28 grams, Carbohydrates: 7 grams, Fat: 18 grams, Saturated Fat: 3 grams, Cholesterol: 65 milligrams, Sodium: 260 milligrams, Fiber: 2 grams, and Sugar: 5 grams.

BAKED MEDITERRANEAN HALIBUT WITH LEMON-CAPER SAUCE

Total Prep Time: 20 minutes
Total Cooking Time: 20-25 minutes
Servings: 4

Ingredients:

Halibut:

- 1 lb (454g) halibut fillets, cut into 4 equal portions
- 2 tablespoons (30ml) olive oil
- 1 tablespoon (15ml) lemon juice
- 2 cloves garlic, minced
- 1 teaspoon (5ml) dried oregano
- Salt and black pepper to taste

Lemon-Caper Sauce:

- 1/4 cup (60ml) lemon juice
- 2 tablespoons (30ml) capers, drained and chopped
- 2 tablespoons (30ml) olive oil
- 1 tablespoon (15ml) Dijon mustard
- 2 cloves garlic, minced
- 2 tablespoons (10g) chopped fresh parsley
- Salt and black pepper to taste

Instructions:

1. Get started by setting your oven temperature to 400°F (200°C).
2. In a shallow baking dish or on a rimmed baking sheet, arrange the halibut fillets in a single layer.
3. Whisk olive oil, lemon juice, garlic, and dried oregano in a small bowl until combined. Season to taste with salt and pepper.
4. Drizzle the oil mixture over the halibut fillets, ensuring they are evenly coated.
5. Carefully slide the baking dish or sheet into the preheated oven. Roast for 20-25 minutes, or until the halibut is cooked through and flaky.

6. Create a zesty sauce by whisking together lemon juice, capers, olive oil, Dijon mustard, and garlic in a small bowl.
7. Stir through chopped parsley, then adjust the seasoning with salt and black pepper to taste.
8. Serve the baked halibut warm, drizzled with the lemon-caper sauce.

Nutritional breakdown per serving:

Calories: 270 kcal, Protein: 27 grams, Carbohydrates: 4 grams, Fat: 15 grams, Saturated Fat: 2 grams, Cholesterol: 55 milligrams, Sodium: 490 milligrams, Fiber: 1 grams, and Sugar: 5 grams.

MEDITERRANEAN-STYLE ROASTED SHRIMP AND VEGETABLES

Total Prep Time: 20 minutes
Total Cooking Time: 25-30 minutes
Servings: 4

Ingredients:

- 1 lb (454g) large shrimp, peeled and deveined
- 2 cups (300g) diced zucchini
- 1 cup (150g) diced bell pepper (any color)
- 1 cup (150g) diced red onion
- 3 cloves garlic, minced
- 2 tablespoons (30ml) olive oil
- 2 tablespoons (30ml) lemon juice
- 1 teaspoon (5ml) dried oregano
- 1/2 teaspoon (2.5ml) dried basil
- 1/4 teaspoon (1.25ml) red pepper flakes (optional)
- Salt and black pepper to taste
- 2 tablespoons (10g) chopped fresh parsley for garnish

Instructions:

1. Get started by setting your oven temperature to 400°F (200°C). Shield a large baking pan by lining it with parchment paper or aluminum foil.
2. Combine shrimp, zucchini, bell pepper, red onion, and garlic in a bowl. Dress with olive oil, lemon juice, oregano, basil, red pepper flakes, salt, and pepper. Toss to coat.
3. Evenly distribute shrimp and vegetables on the baking sheet.
4. Roast until shrimp are cooked and vegetables are tender, about 25-30 minutes.
5. Take the baking sheet out of the oven and transfer the shrimp and vegetables to a serving dish.
6. Top with fresh parsley and serve immediately.

Nutritional breakdown per serving:

Calories: 210 kcal, Protein: 22 grams, Carbohydrates: 11 grams, Fat: 9 grams, Saturated Fat: 1 grams, Cholesterol: 170 milligrams, Sodium: 460 milligrams, Fiber: 3 grams, and Sugar: 5 grams.

MEDITERRANEAN TUNA AND WHITE BEAN SALAD LETTUCE WRAPS

Total Prep Time: 15 minutes
Total Cooking Time: 0 minutes
Servings: 4

Ingredients:

- 2 (5 oz/142g) cans tuna, drained and flaked
- 1 (15 oz/425g) can white beans, rinsed and drained
- 1/2 cup (75g) diced cucumber
- 1/4 cup (35g) diced red onion
- 2 tablespoons (30ml) lemon juice
- 2 tablespoons (30ml) olive oil
- 1 tablespoon (15ml) red wine vinegar
- 1 teaspoon (5ml) dried oregano
- 1/4 teaspoon (1.25ml) red pepper flakes (optional)
- Salt and black pepper to taste
- 8 large lettuce leaves (such as romaine or bibb)

Instructions:

1. Combine tuna, drained white beans, diced cucumber, and red onion in a bowl.
2. Whip up a dressing with lemon juice, olive oil, red wine vinegar, oregano, and red pepper flakes. Season to taste.
3. Drizzle dressing over tuna and beans. Toss gently to coat.
4. Place the tuna and bean salad in the center of each lettuce leaf.
5. Create lettuce cups by folding the leaves around the filling. Serve at once.

Nutritional breakdown per serving:

Calories: 200 kcal, Protein: 18 grams, Carbohydrates: 15 grams, Fat: 8 grams, Saturated Fat: 1 grams, Cholesterol: 25 milligrams, Sodium: 480 milligrams, Fiber: 5 grams, and Sugar: 5 grams.

BAKED MEDITERRANEAN TILAPIA WITH TOMATO-OLIVE TOPPING

Total Prep Time: 15 minutes
Total Cooking Time: 20-25 minutes
Servings: 4

Ingredients:

Tilapia:

- 4 (6 oz/170g) tilapia fillets
- 2 tablespoons (30ml) olive oil
- 2 cloves garlic, minced
- 1 teaspoon (5ml) dried oregano
- Salt and black pepper to taste

Tomato-Olive Topping:

- 1 cup (150g) diced tomatoes
- 1/4 cup (35g) pitted and sliced Kalamata olives
- 2 tablespoons (30ml) chopped fresh basil
- 1 tablespoon (15ml) lemon juice
- 1 tablespoon (15ml) olive oil
- 1 clove garlic, minced
- Salt and black pepper to taste

Instructions:

1. Get started by setting your oven temperature to 400°F (200°C). Lightly grease a baking dish or line a baking sheet with parchment paper.
2. Position the tilapia fillets within the prepared baking dish or on the baking sheet.
3. Combine olive oil, minced garlic, dried oregano, salt, and black pepper in a small bowl.
4. Distribute the seasoning mixture evenly over the fish.
5. Roast the tilapia until cooked through, about 20-25 minutes, or until it reaches an internal temperature of 145°F.
6. Create a fresh salsa by combining diced tomatoes, sliced Kalamata olives, chopped basil, lemon juice, olive oil, and garlic in a small bowl.

7. Season with salt and black pepper to taste.
8. Season generously with salt and pepper.

Nutritional breakdown per serving:

Calories: 240 kcal, Protein: 26 grams, Carbohydrates: 8 grams, Fat: 12 grams, Saturated Fat: 2 grams, Cholesterol: 70 milligrams, Sodium: 580 milligrams, Fiber: 2 grams, and Sugar: 5 grams.

GRILLED MEDITERRANEAN SWORDFISH STEAKS WITH LEMON-HERB GREMOLATA

Total Prep Time: 20 minutes
Total Cooking Time: 10-12 minutes
Servings: 4

Ingredients:

Swordfish Steaks:

- 4 (6 oz/170g) swordfish steaks
- 2 tablespoons (30ml) olive oil
- 1 teaspoon (5ml) dried oregano
- 1/2 teaspoon (2.5ml) paprika
- Salt and black pepper to taste

Lemon-Herb Gremolata:

- 1/4 cup (35g) chopped fresh parsley
- 2 tablespoons (30ml) chopped fresh basil
- 1 tablespoon (15ml) grated lemon zest
- 1 tablespoon (15ml) lemon juice
- 1 clove garlic, minced
- 2 tablespoons (30ml) olive oil
- Salt and black pepper to taste

Instructions:

1. Thoroughly dry the swordfish steaks with paper towels.
2. Prepare a simple seasoning mixture by blending olive oil, dried oregano, paprika, salt, and pepper in a small bowl.
3. Pat the seasoning rub onto both sides of the swordfish steaks.
4. Create a vibrant herb sauce by whisking together chopped parsley, basil, lemon zest, lemon juice, garlic, and olive oil.
5. Add salt and pepper as desired.
6. Get your grill or grill pan hot. Aim for medium-high heat.
7. Grill the swordfish steaks until they are opaque and flake easily with a fork, about 5-6 minutes per side.

8. Serve the grilled swordfish steaks warm, topped with the lemon-herb gremolata.

Nutritional breakdown per serving:

Calories: 280 kcal, Protein: 30 grams, Carbohydrates: 4 grams, Fat: 15 grams, Saturated Fat: 2 grams, Cholesterol: 60 milligrams, Sodium: 430 milligrams, Fiber: 1 grams, and Sugar: 5 grams.

MEDITERRANEAN SHRIMP AND FETA STUFFED PORTOBELLO MUSHROOMS

Total Prep Time: 25 minutes
Total Cooking Time: 20-25 minutes
Servings: 4

Ingredients:

Stuffed Portobello Mushrooms:

- 4 large portobello mushroom caps, stems removed, chopped
- 1 tablespoon (15ml) olive oil
- 1/2 cup (75g) diced onion
- 2 cloves garlic, minced
- 1 lb (454g) peeled and deveined shrimp, chopped
- 1/4 cup (35g) crumbled feta cheese
- 2 tablespoons (30ml) chopped fresh parsley
- 1 teaspoon (5ml) dried oregano
- Salt and black pepper to taste

Topping:

- 1/4 cup (35g) breadcrumbs
- 2 tablespoons (30ml) grated Parmesan cheese
- 1 tablespoon (15ml) olive oil

Instructions:

1. Get started by setting your oven temperature to 400°F (200°C). Prepare baking sheet by greasing or lining with parchment paper.

2. Prepare the portobello mushrooms:
    - Remove and finely chop mushroom stems.
    - Position mushroom caps on prepared baking sheet.

3. Make the shrimp and feta filling:
    - Gently heat olive oil in a pan over medium heat.

- Add the chopped onion and sauté for 2-3 minutes until translucent.
- Stir in the minced garlic and chopped mushroom stems, and sauté for an additional minute.
- Add the chopped shrimp and cook for 3-4 minutes, until the shrimp are opaque and cooked through.
- Take the skillet off the heat and blend in crumbled feta, chopped parsley, dried oregano, salt, and pepper.

4. Stuff the portobello mushrooms:

- Evenly distribute the shrimp and feta filling into the portobello mushroom caps.

5. Make the topping:

- In a small bowl, whisk together breadcrumbs, Parmesan cheese, and olive oil.
- Sprinkle the topping evenly over the stuffed portobello mushrooms.

6. Bake the stuffed mushrooms:

- Bake the tray in the preheated oven for 20-25 minutes, or until the mushrooms are soft and the topping turns golden.

7. Serve the Mediterranean Shrimp and Feta Stuffed Portobello Mushrooms warm.

Nutritional breakdown per serving:

Calories: 310 kcal, Protein: 26 grams, Carbohydrates: 14 grams, Fat: 16 grams, Saturated Fat: 5 grams, Cholesterol: 190 milligrams, Sodium: 680 milligrams, Fiber: 3 grams, and Sugar: 5 grams.

BAKED MEDITERRANEAN SEA BASS WITH ROASTED VEGETABLES

Total Prep Time: 25 minutes
Total Cooking Time: 30-35 minutes
Servings: 4

Ingredients:

Roasted Vegetables:

- 2 cups (280g) diced zucchini
- 1 cup (150g) diced red bell pepper
- 1 cup (150g) diced eggplant
- 1 cup (150g) diced red onion
- 2 tablespoons (30ml) olive oil
- 1 teaspoon (5ml) dried oregano
- Salt and black pepper to taste

Sea Bass:

- 4 (6 oz/170g) sea bass fillets
- 2 tablespoons (30ml) olive oil
- 1 teaspoon (5ml) lemon zest
- 2 tablespoons (30ml) lemon juice
- 2 cloves garlic, minced
- 1 teaspoon (5ml) dried oregano
- Salt and black pepper to taste

Garnish:

- 2 tablespoons (30ml) chopped fresh parsley
- 1 lemon, cut into wedges

Instructions:

1. Get started by setting your oven temperature to 400°F (200°C). Prepare baking sheet by greasing or lining with parchment paper.

2. Prepare the roasted vegetables:

- In a large bowl, combine diced zucchini, red bell pepper, eggplant, and red onion. Drizzle with olive oil, then season with dried oregano, salt, and pepper. Toss gently to coat.
- Create a single layer of vegetables on the prepared baking sheet.
- Bake the vegetables for 20-25 minutes, or until softened and lightly golden, tossing them halfway through.

3. Prepare the sea bass:

- Remove excess moisture from the sea bass fillets using paper towels.
- Mix olive oil, finely grated lemon peel, lemon juice, chopped garlic, dried oregano, salt, and black pepper in a small bowl.
- Brush the sea bass fillets with the lemon-herb mixture, ensuring they are evenly coated.

4. Bake the sea bass:

- Adjust the oven temperature down to 375°F (190°C).
- Arrange the seasoned sea bass fillets on the baking sheet alongside the roasted vegetables.
- Roast the dish for 10-12 minutes, or until the sea bass is opaque and easily flakes apart with a fork.

5. Present the Baked Mediterranean Sea Bass accompanied by the roasted vegetables. Top it off with a garnish of chopped fresh parsley and lemon wedges.

Nutritional breakdown per serving:

Calories: 320 kcal, Protein: 34 grams, Carbohydrates: 15 grams, Fat: 15 grams, Saturated Fat: 2 grams, Cholesterol: 60 milligrams, Sodium: 360 milligrams, Fiber: 5 grams, and Sugar: 5 grams.

GRILLED MEDITERRANEAN MAHI-MAHI SKEWERS WITH PINEAPPLE SALSA

Total Prep Time: 30 minutes
Total Cooking Time: 12-15 minutes
Servings: 4

Ingredients:

Mahi-Mahi Skewers:

- 1 lb (454g) mahi-mahi fillets, cut into 1-inch cubes
- 2 tablespoons (30ml) olive oil
- 1 tablespoon (15ml) lemon juice
- 1 teaspoon (5ml) dried oregano
- 1/2 teaspoon (2.5ml) paprika
- Salt and black pepper to taste

Pineapple Salsa:

- 1 cup (150g) diced fresh pineapple
- 1/2 cup (75g) diced red onion
- 1/4 cup (35g) diced red bell pepper
- 2 tablespoons (30ml) chopped fresh cilantro
- 1 tablespoon (15ml) lime juice
- 1 teaspoon (5ml) minced jalapeño (optional, for heat)
- Salt and black pepper to taste

Instructions:

1. Let 8-10 wooden skewers soak in water for a minimum of 30 minutes. This step helps ensure the skewers don't burn during cooking.

2. Prepare the mahi-mahi skewers:

    - Gather the diced pineapple, red onion, red bell pepper, chopped cilantro, lime juice, and minced jalapeño (if using) in a medium-sized bowl. Combine these ingredients together.
    - Thread the seasoned mahi-mahi cubes onto the soaked wooden skewers.

3. Make the pineapple salsa:

   - In a medium bowl, combine the diced pineapple, red onion, red bell pepper, chopped cilantro, lime juice, and minced jalapeño (if using).
   - Finish the salsa by seasoning it with salt and black pepper to your desired taste.

4. Grill the mahi-mahi skewers:

   - Start by setting your grill or grill pan to a medium-high heat level.
   - Grill the mahi-mahi skewers for 6-8 minutes, turning occasionally, until the fish is opaque and flakes easily with a fork.

5. Serve the grilled mahi-mahi skewers warm, topped with the pineapple salsa.

Nutritional breakdown per serving:

Calories: 260 kcal, Protein: 28 grams, Carbohydrates: 14 grams, Fat: 10 grams, Saturated Fat: 2 grams, Cholesterol: 90 milligrams, Sodium: 370 milligrams, Fiber: 2 grams, and Sugar: 5 grams.

MEDITERRANEAN TUNA-STUFFED TOMATOES

Total Prep Time: 20 minutes
Total Cooking Time: 15 minutes
Servings: 4

Ingredients:

- 4 large tomatoes
- 1 (5 oz/142g) can tuna, drained and flaked
- 1/4 cup (35g) crumbled feta cheese
- 2 tablespoons (30ml) chopped fresh parsley
- 2 tablespoons (30ml) chopped fresh basil
- 1 tablespoon (15ml) lemon juice
- 1 clove garlic, minced
- 1 tablespoon (15ml) olive oil
- Salt and black pepper to taste

Instructions:

1. Get started by setting your oven temperature to 375°F (190°C).
2. Begin by slicing the tops off the tomatoes. Next, gently scoop out the insides, ensuring a thin shell remains. Finally, finely chop the removed tomato pulp.
3. In a medium-sized bowl, gather the chopped tomato pulp, tuna, feta cheese, parsley, basil, lemon juice, garlic, and olive oil. Combine these ingredients together and season with salt and black pepper to taste.
4. Stuff the tuna mixture into the hollowed-out tomato shells, packing it in gently.
5. Arrange the stuffed tomatoes on a baking sheet and place them in the oven. Bake for 12-15 minutes, or until the tomatoes are heated through and the filling is hot.
6. Serve the Mediterranean Tuna-Stuffed Tomatoes warm.

Nutritional breakdown per serving:

Calories: 150 kcal, Protein: 13 grams, Carbohydrates: 9 grams, Fat: 8 grams, Saturated Fat: 2 grams, Cholesterol: 30 milligrams, Sodium: 350 milligrams, Fiber: 2 grams, and Sugar: 5 grams.

BAKED MEDITERRANEAN SALMON CAKES WITH TZATZIKI SAUCE

Total Prep Time: 30 minutes
Total Cooking Time: 20 minutes
Servings: 4

Ingredients:

Salmon Cakes:

- 1 lb (454g) salmon fillets, cooked and flaked
- 1/2 cup (75g) panko breadcrumbs
- 1/4 cup (35g) crumbled feta cheese
- 2 tablespoons (30ml) chopped fresh parsley
- 1 tablespoon (15ml) lemon juice
- 1 clove garlic, minced
- 1 egg, beaten
- Salt and black pepper to taste

Tzatziki Sauce:

- 1 cup (240g) plain Greek yogurt
- 1/2 grated cucumber, drained
- 1 clove garlic, minced
- 1 tablespoon (15ml) lemon juice
- 2 tablespoons (30ml) chopped fresh dill
- Salt and black pepper to taste

Instructions:

1. Get started by setting your oven temperature to 400°F (200°C). Line a baking sheet with parchment paper.

2. Make the salmon cakes:
   - Combine flaked salmon, panko, feta, parsley, lemon juice, minced garlic, and beaten egg in a medium bowl. Stir gently to blend. Season with salt and black pepper.

- Divide the mixture into 8 portions and mold each into a patty about 3 inches across and half an inch deep.
- Place the salmon cakes on the prepared baking sheet.

3. Prepare the tzatziki sauce:

- Gather a small bowl and combine the Greek yogurt, grated and drained cucumber, minced garlic, lemon juice, and chopped dill. Finally, season the combined ingredients with salt and black pepper to your preferred taste.

4. Bake the salmon cakes:

- Place the salmon cakes in the preheated oven and bake them for 15-20 minutes, or until they are lightly golden in color and cooked through.

5. Serve the baked Mediterranean salmon cakes warm, with the tzatziki sauce on the side.

Nutritional breakdown per serving:

Calories: 320 kcal, Protein: 28 grams, Carbohydrates: 16 grams, Fat: 15 grams, Saturated Fat: 5 grams, Cholesterol: 100 milligrams, Sodium: 550 milligrams, Fiber: 1 grams, and Sugar: 5 grams.

GRILLED MEDITERRANEAN SWORDFISH AND VEGETABLE FOIL PACKETS

Total Prep Time: 25 minutes
Total Cooking Time: 20 minutes
Servings: 4

Ingredients:

- 1 lb (454g) swordfish fillets, cut into 4 equal-sized pieces
- 2 cups (300g) diced zucchini
- 1 cup (150g) diced red bell pepper
- 1 cup (150g) diced red onion
- 2 tablespoons (30ml) olive oil
- 2 tablespoons (30ml) lemon juice
- 1 tablespoon (15ml) chopped fresh oregano
- 1 tablespoon (15ml) chopped fresh parsley
- 2 cloves garlic, minced
- Salt and black pepper to taste

Instructions:

1. Preheat your grill to medium-high heat.
2. Cut four lengths of heavy-duty aluminum foil, each about 12 inches long.
3. Toss diced zucchini, red bell pepper, and red onion with olive oil, lemon juice, oregano, parsley, and garlic in a large bowl. Season generously with salt and pepper.
4. Divide the vegetable mixture into four equal portions and place one portion in the middle of each foil sheet.
5. Place a piece of swordfish on top of the vegetables in each foil packet.
6. Seal the swordfish and vegetables in the foil packets by folding and crimping the edges.
7. Place the sealed foil packets on the hot grill. Cook for 15-20 minutes, or until the swordfish is cooked and the vegetables are tender.
8. Gently remove the packets from the grill and let them cool slightly before unfolding.
9. Serve the Grilled Mediterranean Swordfish and Vegetable Foil Packets immediately.

Nutritional breakdown per serving:

Calories: 260 kcal, Protein: 26 grams, Carbohydrates: 12 grams, Fat: 12 grams, Saturated Fat: 2 grams, Cholesterol: 60 milligrams, Sodium: 250 milligrams, Fiber: 3 grams, and Sugar: 5 grams.

MEDITERRANEAN BAKED COD WITH ARTICHOKE AND OLIVE TAPENADE

Total Prep Time: 20 minutes
Total Cooking Time: 25 minutes
Servings: 4

Ingredients:

Artichoke and Olive Tapenade:

- 1 (14 oz or 400g) can artichoke hearts, drained and chopped
- 1/2 cup (75g) pitted kalamata olives, chopped
- 2 tablespoons (30ml) olive oil
- 2 tablespoons (30ml) lemon juice
- 2 cloves garlic, minced
- 2 tablespoons (30ml) chopped fresh parsley
- Salt and black pepper to taste

Baked Cod:

- 4 (6 oz or 170g) cod fillets
- 2 tablespoons (30ml) olive oil
- 2 tablespoons (30ml) lemon juice
- 1 teaspoon (5ml) dried oregano
- Salt and black pepper to taste

Instructions:

1. Get started by setting your oven temperature to 400°F (200°C). Line a baking sheet with parchment paper.

2. Make the artichoke and olive tapenade:
   - Toss chopped artichoke hearts, kalamata olives, olive oil, lemon juice, minced garlic, and parsley together in a medium bowl. Season generously with salt and pepper.

3. Prepare the baked cod:
   - Position the cod fillets on the prepared baking tray.

- Top the cod with a drizzle of olive oil and lemon juice. Season to taste with dried oregano, salt, and pepper.

4. Bake the cod:

- Roast the cod in the preheated oven until cooked and flaky, about 18 to 22 minutes.

5. Serve the baked cod warm, topped with the artichoke and olive tapenade.

Nutritional breakdown per serving:

Calories: 290 kcal, Protein: 30 grams, Carbohydrates: 10 grams, Fat: 14 grams, Saturated Fat: 2 grams, Cholesterol: 70 milligrams, Sodium: 600 milligrams, Fiber: 4 grams, and Sugar: 5 grams.

MEDITERRANEAN SHRIMP ORZO SALAD WITH FETA AND HERBS

Total Prep Time: 30 minutes
Total Cooking Time: 20 minutes
Servings: 4

Ingredients:

- 1 cup (170g) uncooked orzo pasta
- 1 lb (450g) cooked shrimp, peeled and deveined
- 1 cup (150g) diced cucumber
- 1 cup (150g) cherry tomatoes, halved
- 1/2 cup (75g) crumbled feta cheese
- 1/4 cup (40g) pitted kalamata olives, sliced
- 2 tablespoons (30ml) chopped fresh parsley
- 2 tablespoons (30ml) chopped fresh basil
- 2 tablespoons (30ml) lemon juice
- 2 tablespoons (30ml) olive oil
- 1 clove garlic, minced
- Salt and black pepper to taste

Instructions:

1. Cook orzo as instructed on the package. Drain completely and refresh under cold water.
2. Toss together cooked, cooled orzo, cooked shrimp, diced cucumber, cherry tomatoes, crumbled feta, and sliced kalamata olives in a large bowl.
3. In a small bowl, whisk together the chopped parsley, chopped basil, lemon juice, olive oil, and minced garlic. Season generously with salt and pepper.
4. Pour the dressing onto the orzo salad and toss lightly to coat.
5. Refrigerate the salad for at least 15 minutes to allow the flavors to blend.
6. Serve chilled or at room temperature.

Nutritional breakdown per serving:

Calories: 320 kcal, Protein: 24 grams, Carbohydrates: 25 grams, Fat: 14 grams, Saturated Fat: 4 grams, Cholesterol: 170 milligrams, Sodium: 650 milligrams, Fiber: 3 grams, and Sugar: 5 grams.

GRILLED MEDITERRANEAN SNAPPER WITH ROASTED GARLIC HUMMUS

Grilled Mediterranean Snapper
Total Cooking Time: 30 minutes
Prep Time: 15 minutes
Servings: 4

Ingredients:

- 4 (6-ounce) snapper fillets
- 2 tablespoons olive oil
- 1 tablespoon lemon juice
- 1 teaspoon dried oregano
- 1/2 teaspoon salt
- 1/4 teaspoon black pepper
- 1 lemon, cut into wedges for serving

Directions:

1. Preheat the grill to medium-high heat.
2. Prepare a marinade by blending olive oil, lemon juice, oregano, salt, and pepper in a shallow dish. Add snapper fillets and coat evenly on both sides.
3. Grill the snapper fillets for 3 to 4 minutes per side, or until they flake easily with a fork.
4. Serve the grilled snapper warm, with lemon wedges on the side.

Nutritional breakdown per serving:

Calories: 220 kcal, Protein: 30 grams, Carbohydrates: 2 grams, Fat: 10 grams, Saturated Fat: 3 grams, Cholesterol: 60 milligrams, Sodium: 480 milligrams, Fiber: 0 grams, and Sugar: 0 grams.

ROASTED GARLIC HUMMUS

Total Prep Time: 30 minutes
Servings: 8 (1/4 cup per serving)

Ingredients:

- 1 head of garlic
- 1 (15-ounce) can chickpeas, drained and rinsed
- 1/4 cup tahini
- 2 tablespoons lemon juice
- 2 tablespoons olive oil
- 1/2 teaspoon salt
- 1/4 teaspoon ground cumin
- 2-3 tablespoons water (as needed)

Directions:

1. Get started by setting your oven temperature to 400°F (200°C).
2. Cut the top off the head of garlic to expose the cloves. Top with a small amount of olive oil and cover with foil.
3. Place the garlic in a preheated oven and bake until tender and fragrant, approximately 30-40 minutes. Let cool down a bit.
4. Pulse roasted garlic cloves, chickpeas, tahini, lemon juice, olive oil, salt, and cumin together in a food processor. Process until smooth, adding water as needed to achieve the desired consistency.
5. Transfer the roasted garlic hummus to a serving bowl and serve with the grilled Mediterranean snapper.

Nutritional breakdown per serving:

Calories: 120 kcal, Protein: 4 grams, Carbohydrates: 10 grams, Fat: 8 grams, Saturated Fat: 1 grams, Cholesterol: 0 milligrams, Sodium: 280 milligrams, Fiber: 3 grams, and Sugar: 5 grams.

BAKED MEDITERRANEAN HALIBUT WITH TOMATO-BASIL RELISH

Total Cooking Time: 35 minutes
Prep Time: 15 minutes
Servings: 4

Ingredients:

- 4 (6-ounce) halibut fillets
- 2 tablespoons olive oil
- 1 tablespoon lemon juice
- 1 teaspoon dried oregano
- 1/2 teaspoon salt
- 1/4 teaspoon black pepper
- 1/4 cup panko breadcrumbs
- 2 tablespoons grated Parmesan cheese

Tomato-Basil Relish:

- 1 cup diced Roma tomatoes
- 1/4 cup finely chopped fresh basil
- 2 tablespoons diced red onion
- 1 tablespoon olive oil
- 1 tablespoon balsamic vinegar
- 1/4 teaspoon salt
- 1/8 teaspoon black pepper

Directions:

1. Get started by setting your oven temperature to 400°F (200°C).
2. Whisk together olive oil, lemon juice, oregano, salt, and pepper in a small bowl.
3. Position the halibut fillets in a baking dish. Distribute the oil mixture evenly over the fish.
4. Create a mixture of panko and Parmesan in a small bowl. Scatter it evenly over the halibut.
5. Cook the halibut in the oven for 18-22 minutes, or until cooked and the topping is lightly browned.

6. Simultaneously, create a tomato-basil relish. In a medium bowl, mix together diced tomatoes, chopped basil, diced onion, olive oil, balsamic vinegar, salt, and pepper.
7. Serve the baked halibut warm, topped with the Tomato-Basil Relish.

Nutritional breakdown per serving:

Calories: 320 kcal, Protein: 33 grams, Carbohydrates: 12 grams, Fat: 16 grams, Saturated Fat: 3 grams, Cholesterol: 60 milligrams, Sodium: 750 milligrams, Fiber: 2 grams, and Sugar: 9 grams.

MEDITERRANEAN TUNA STUFFED AVOCADO BOATS

Total Prep Time: 20 minutes
Servings: 4 (2 halves per serving)

Ingredients:

- 2 large ripe avocados, halved and pits removed
- 1 (5-ounce) can tuna, drained
- 2 tablespoons diced red onion
- 2 tablespoons diced cucumber
- 2 tablespoons crumbled feta cheese
- 1 tablespoon chopped fresh parsley
- 1 tablespoon olive oil
- 1 tablespoon lemon juice
- 1/4 teaspoon dried oregano
- 1/4 teaspoon salt
- 1/8 teaspoon black pepper

Directions:

1. Carefully scoop out the avocado flesh, leaving a quarter-inch thick shell intact to form "boats." Dice the scooped-out avocado flesh and set aside.
2. In a medium bowl, bring together drained tuna, diced avocado, red onion, cucumber, crumbled feta, and parsley.
3. Whisk olive oil, lemon juice, oregano, salt, and pepper together in a small bowl to form a vinaigrette.
4. Add the dressing to the tuna and avocado mixture and stir gently to combine.
5. Spoon the tuna-avocado mixture evenly into the avocado boats.
6. Serve the stuffed avocado boats immediately.

Nutritional breakdown per serving:

Calories: 260 kcal, Protein: 15 grams, Carbohydrates: 12 grams, Fat: 18 grams, Saturated Fat: 4 grams, Cholesterol: 25 milligrams, Sodium: 370 milligrams, Fiber: 7 grams, and Sugar: 1 grams.

GRILLED MEDITERRANEAN SALMON SKEWERS WITH PESTO DRIZZLE

Total Cooking Time: 25 minutes
Prep Time: 20 minutes
Servings: 4 (2 skewers per serving)

Ingredients:

Salmon Skewers:

- 1 lb salmon fillet, cut into 1-inch cubes
- 1 tablespoon olive oil
- 1 teaspoon dried oregano
- 1/2 teaspoon salt
- 1/4 teaspoon black pepper

Pesto Drizzle:

- 1/2 cup fresh basil leaves
- 2 tablespoons pine nuts
- 2 tablespoons grated Parmesan cheese
- 1 tablespoon olive oil
- 1 garlic clove, minced
- 1/4 teaspoon salt

Skewer Ingredients:

- 1 cup cherry tomatoes
- 1 cup cubed zucchini
- 1/2 cup pitted Kalamata olives, halved

Directions:

1. In a medium bowl, combine the cubed salmon, olive oil, oregano, salt, and black pepper. Toss to coat the salmon evenly.
2. For the Pesto Drizzle, in a food processor, combine the basil, pine nuts, Parmesan, olive oil, garlic, and salt. Blend until a smooth pesto forms. Set aside.
3. Thread the salmon cubes, cherry tomatoes, zucchini cubes, and Kalamata olive halves onto skewers, alternating the ingredients.

4. Turn on your grill or grill pan and preheat it to medium-high temperature.
5. Grill the salmon skewers for 8-10 minutes, turning occasionally, until the salmon is cooked through and flakes easily with a fork.
6. Arrange the grilled salmon skewers on a serving platter. Drizzle the Pesto Drizzle over the top.
7. Serve the salmon skewers immediately.

Nutritional breakdown per serving (2 skewers):

Calories: 330 kcal, Protein: 26 grams, Carbohydrates: 9 grams, Fat: 22 grams, Saturated Fat: 4 grams, Cholesterol: 70 milligrams, Sodium: 580 milligrams, Fiber: 3 grams, and Sugar: 4 grams.

BAKED MEDITERRANEAN COD WITH ROASTED RED PEPPER SAUCE

Total Cooking Time: 40 minutes
Prep Time: 20 minutes
Servings: 4

Ingredients:

Cod:

- 4 (6-ounce) cod fillets
- 2 tablespoons olive oil
- 1 teaspoon dried oregano
- 1/2 teaspoon garlic powder
- 1/4 teaspoon salt
- 1/4 teaspoon black pepper

Roasted Red Pepper Sauce:

- 2 red bell peppers, roasted and peeled
- 1/4 cup olive oil
- 2 tablespoons chopped fresh parsley
- 2 tablespoons lemon juice
- 1 garlic clove, minced
- 1/4 teaspoon salt
- 1/8 teaspoon black pepper

Garnish:

- 2 tablespoons crumbled feta cheese
- 2 tablespoons chopped fresh parsley

Directions:

1. Get started by setting your oven temperature to 400°F (200°C).
2. Whisk together olive oil, oregano, garlic powder, salt, and pepper in a small bowl.
3. Position the cod fillets in a baking dish, then coat the tops with the oil mixture.
4. Place the cod in the oven and bake for 15-20 minutes, or until flaky.

5. While the cod is baking, prepare the Roasted Red Pepper Sauce. Roast the bell peppers directly over a flame or under a broiler, turning regularly until the skin is charred. Transfer the roasted peppers to a bowl, seal it with plastic wrap, and let them sit for 10 minutes. Peel off the skin, remove the seeds, and chop the peppers.
6. Process roasted red peppers, olive oil, parsley, lemon juice, garlic, salt, and pepper in a blender or food processor until completely smooth.
7. Serve the baked cod warm, topped with the Roasted Red Pepper Sauce, crumbled feta cheese, and chopped parsley.

Nutritional breakdown per serving:

Calories: 320 kcal, Protein: 32 grams, Carbohydrates: 9 grams, Fat: 28 grams, Saturated Fat: 5 grams, Cholesterol: 70 milligrams, Sodium: 620 milligrams, Fiber: 3 grams, and Sugar: 4 grams.

MEDITERRANEAN SHRIMP AND FETA STUFFED ZUCCHINI BOATS

Total Cooking Time: 40 minutes
Prep Time: 20 minutes
Servings: 4 (2 stuffed zucchini halves per serving)

Ingredients:

- 4 medium zucchini, halved lengthwise
- 1 tablespoon olive oil
- 1/2 cup diced onion
- 2 garlic cloves, minced
- 1 lb peeled and deveined shrimp, chopped
- 1/2 cup crumbled feta cheese
- 2 tablespoons chopped fresh parsley
- 1 tablespoon lemon juice
- 1 teaspoon dried oregano
- 1/4 teaspoon crushed red pepper flakes
- 1/4 teaspoon salt
- 1/8 teaspoon black pepper

Topping:

- 2 tablespoons panko breadcrumbs
- 1 tablespoon grated Parmesan cheese

Directions:

1. Get started by setting your oven temperature to 375°F (190°C).
2. Scoop out the zucchini's insides, leaving a quarter-inch thick base. Finely chop the scooped-out zucchini flesh.
3. Place a large skillet over medium heat. Add olive oil. Soften diced onion and minced garlic in the hot oil for 2-3 minutes.
4. Add the chopped zucchini flesh and shrimp to the skillet. Cook the shrimp for approximately 5-6 minutes, stirring regularly, until it turns opaque and is cooked through.
5. Take the skillet off the heat. Incorporate crumbled feta, chopped parsley, lemon juice, dried oregano, red pepper flakes, salt, and pepper.

6. Spoon the shrimp and feta mixture evenly into the zucchini boats.
7. Mix panko breadcrumbs with grated Parmesan cheese in a small bowl. Sprinkle the topping over the stuffed zucchini boats.
8. Bake the stuffed zucchini boats for 18-20 minutes, or until the zucchini is tender and the topping is golden brown.
9. Serve the Mediterranean Shrimp and Feta Stuffed Zucchini Boats warm.

Nutritional breakdown per serving (2 stuffed zucchini halves):

Calories: 250 kcal, Protein: 23 grams, Carbohydrates: 14 grams, Fat: 21 grams, Saturated Fat: 5 grams, Cholesterol: 165 milligrams, Sodium: 530 milligrams, Fiber: 3 grams, and Sugar: 6 grams.

CHAPTER 4
SALADS, SIDES, AND VEGETARIAN DELIGHTS

ROASTED MEDITERRANEAN VEGETABLE MEDLEY

Total Cooking Time: 50 minutes
Prep Time: 15 minutes
Servings: 6

Ingredients:

- 1 eggplant, cut into 1-inch cubes
- 1 zucchini, cut into 1-inch cubes
- 1 red bell pepper, cut into chunks
- 1 yellow onion, cut into 1-inch wedges
- 3 garlic cloves, minced
- 2 tablespoons olive oil
- 1 teaspoon dried oregano
- 1 teaspoon dried basil
- 1/2 teaspoon salt
- 1/4 teaspoon black pepper
- 1/4 cup crumbled feta cheese
- 2 tablespoons chopped fresh parsley

Directions:

1. Get started by setting your oven temperature to 400°F (200°C).
2. Combine the diced eggplant, zucchini, bell pepper, and onion wedges in a spacious mixing bowl.
3. Add the minced garlic, olive oil, dried oregano, dried basil, salt, and black pepper. Gently combine all the vegetables until coated completely.
4. Distribute the seasoned vegetables evenly in a single layer on a parchment-lined baking sheet.
5. Bake the vegetables for 35-40 minutes in a preheated oven, stirring them midway.
6. Once the vegetables are roasted, take them out of the oven and put them in a serving bowl.
7. Garnish the roasted vegetables with crumbled feta cheese and chopped fresh parsley.
8. Serve the Roasted Mediterranean Vegetable Medley warm.

Nutritional breakdown per serving:

Calories: 120 kcal, Protein: 3 grams, Carbohydrates: 14 grams, Fat: 7 grams, Saturated Fat: 2 grams, Cholesterol: 10 milligrams, Sodium: 280 milligrams, Fiber: 5 grams, and Sugar: 6 grams.

MEDITERRANEAN QUINOA AND VEGETABLE STUFFED PORTOBELLO MUSHROOMS

Total Cooking Time: 45 minutes
Prep Time: 20 minutes
Servings: 4 (2 stuffed mushrooms per serving)

Ingredients:

- 8 large portobello mushroom caps, stems finely chopped
- 1 cup cooked quinoa
- 1 cup diced tomatoes
- 1/2 cup crumbled feta cheese
- 1/2 cup diced cucumber
- 1/4 cup diced red onion
- 2 tablespoons chopped fresh basil
- 1 tablespoon lemon juice
- 1 teaspoon olive oil
- 1/2 teaspoon dried oregano
- 1/4 teaspoon salt
- 1/8 teaspoon black pepper

Topping:

- 2 tablespoons panko breadcrumbs
- 1 tablespoon grated Parmesan cheese

Directions:

1. Get started by setting your oven temperature to 400°F (200°C).
2. In a large bowl, combine the finely chopped mushroom stems, cooked quinoa, diced tomatoes, crumbled feta cheese, diced cucumber, diced red onion, chopped fresh basil, lemon juice, olive oil, dried oregano, salt, and black pepper. Combine ingredients thoroughly.
3. Arrange the portobello mushroom caps, gill-side up, on a baking sheet lined with parchment paper.
4. Distribute the quinoa mixture evenly among the mushroom caps, pressing lightly.
5. Combine panko and Parmesan in a bowl. Sprinkle over the stuffed mushrooms.

6. Bake until the mushrooms are tender and the topping achieves a golden brown crust, about 20-25 minutes.
7. Remove from oven and cool for a short time before enjoying.
8. Serve the Mediterranean Quinoa and Vegetable Stuffed Portobello Mushrooms warm.

Nutritional breakdown per serving:

Calories: 200 kcal, Protein: 10 grams, Carbohydrates: 22 grams, Fat: 9 grams, Saturated Fat: 4 grams, Cholesterol: 20 milligrams, Sodium: 450 milligrams, Fiber: 4 grams, and Sugar: 5 grams.

BAKED MEDITERRANEAN RATATOUILLE WITH FETA AND OLIVES

Total Cooking Time: 1 hour 15 minutes
Prep Time: 30 minutes
Servings: 6

Ingredients:

- 1 eggplant, cut into 1-inch cubes
- 1 zucchini, cut into 1-inch rounds
- 1 yellow squash, cut into 1-inch rounds
- 1 red bell pepper, diced
- 1 onion, sliced
- 3 garlic cloves, minced
- 2 tablespoons olive oil
- 1 teaspoon dried oregano
- 1 teaspoon dried basil
- 1/2 teaspoon salt
- 1/4 teaspoon black pepper
- 1 (14.5 oz) can diced tomatoes
- 1/2 cup crumbled feta cheese
- 1/4 cup pitted kalamata olives, halved

Directions:

1. Get started by setting your oven temperature to 375°F (190°C).
2. Toss together the cubed eggplant, zucchini and yellow squash rounds, bell pepper chunks, and sliced onion in a large bowl.
3. Add the minced garlic, olive oil, dried oregano, dried basil, salt, and black pepper. Combine the vegetables until thoroughly mixed.
4. Distribute the seasoned vegetables evenly on a large baking sheet lined with parchment paper.
5. Roast the veggies until tender and browned, about 40-45 minutes, stirring once halfway through.
6. Take the roasted vegetables out of the oven and place them in a large baking dish.
7. Incorporate the diced tomatoes, including their juices, by stirring.
8. Create a topping of crumbled feta and halved kalamata olives for the ratatouille.

9. Return the dish to the oven and bake for an additional 15-20 minutes, or until the feta is melted and the dish is heated through.
10. Serve the Baked Mediterranean Ratatouille with Feta and Olives warm.

Nutritional breakdown per serving:

Calories: 180 kcal, Protein: 6 grams, Carbohydrates: 16 grams, Fat: 12 grams, Saturated Fat: 4 grams, Cholesterol: 20 milligrams, Sodium: 620 milligrams, Fiber: 5 grams, and Sugar: 8 grams.

MEDITERRANEAN CHICKPEA AND VEGETABLE SALAD

Total Cooking Time: 20 minutes
Prep Time: 15 minutes
Servings: 4

Ingredients:

- 15 oz chickpeas, drained
- 1 cup diced cucumber
- 1 cup cherry tomatoes, halved
- 1/2 cup diced red onion
- 1/2 cup crumbled feta cheese
- 1/4 cup pitted kalamata olives, halved
- 2 tablespoons chopped fresh parsley
- 2 tablespoons lemon juice
- 1 tablespoon olive oil
- 1 teaspoon dried oregano
- 1/4 teaspoon salt
- 1/8 teaspoon black pepper

Directions:

1. Toss together chickpeas, diced cucumber, halved cherry tomatoes, red onion, crumbled feta, and halved kalamata olives in a large bowl.
2. In a small bowl, whisk together the chopped fresh parsley, lemon juice, olive oil, dried oregano, salt, and black pepper.
3. Drizzle the dressing over the chickpea and vegetable mixture and toss gently to combine.
4. Refrigerate the covered salad for at least 10 minutes to let the flavors blend.
5. Serve the chilled Mediterranean Chickpea and Vegetable Salad.

Nutritional breakdown per serving:

Calories: 210 kcal, Protein: 8 grams, Carbohydrates: 22 grams, Fat: 11 grams, Saturated Fat: 3 grams, Cholesterol: 15 milligrams, Sodium: 530 milligrams, Fiber: 6 grams, and Sugar: 4 grams.

GRILLED MEDITERRANEAN VEGETABLE SKEWERS WITH ZUCCHINI HUMMUS

Total Cooking Time: 45 minutes
Prep Time: 20 minutes
Servings: 4 (2 skewers per serving)

Ingredients:

Vegetable Skewers:

- 1 red bell pepper, diced
- 1 yellow bell pepper, diced
- 1 medium zucchini, cut into 1-inch rounds
- 1 medium yellow squash, cut into 1-inch rounds
- 1 red onion, cut into 1-inch pieces
- 2 tablespoons olive oil
- 1 teaspoon dried oregano
- 1/2 teaspoon salt
- 1/4 teaspoon black pepper

Zucchini Hummus:

- 1 medium zucchini, grated (about 1 cup)
- 15 oz chickpeas, drained
- 2 tablespoons tahini
- 2 tablespoons lemon juice
- 1 garlic clove, minced
- 1/4 teaspoon ground cumin
- 1/4 teaspoon salt

Directions:

1. Grill or grill pan, preheated to medium-high.
2. In a spacious bowl, combine chopped bell peppers, zucchini, yellow squash, and red onion. Drizzle the salmon cakes generously with olive oil and season them with a sprinkle of dried oregano, salt, and black pepper. Toss gently until all vegetables are evenly coated.

3. Thread the seasoned vegetables onto skewers, leaving a small space between each piece.
4. Place the skewers on the grill and cook for 12 to 15 minutes, turning often to ensure even cooking and the development of desirable char marks.
5. While the skewers are grilling, prepare the zucchini hummus.
6. In a food processor, combine the grated zucchini, drained and rinsed chickpeas, tahini, lemon juice, garlic, ground cumin, and salt. Blend until smooth and creamy.
7. Spoon the zucchini hummus into a serving dish.
8. Serve the grilled Mediterranean vegetable skewers warm, with the zucchini hummus on the side for dipping.

Nutritional breakdown per serving:

Calories: 260 kcal, Protein: 9 grams, Carbohydrates: 27 grams, Fat: 15 grams, Saturated Fat: 2 grams, Cholesterol: 0 milligrams, Sodium: 720 milligrams, Fiber: 8 grams, and Sugar: 8 grams.

BAKED MEDITERRANEAN FETA AND VEGETABLE STUFFED TOMATOES

Total Cooking Time: 45 minutes
Prep Time: 20 minutes
Servings: 6 (2 stuffed tomatoes per serving)

Ingredients:

- 12 medium-sized tomatoes
- 1 cup diced zucchini
- 1/2 cup diced red onion
- 1/2 cup diced red bell pepper
- 1/4 cup crumbled feta cheese
- 2 tablespoons chopped fresh basil
- 1 tablespoon olive oil
- 1 garlic clove, minced
- 1/4 teaspoon salt
- 1/8 teaspoon black pepper

Directions:

1. Get started by setting your oven temperature to 375°F (190°C).
2. Remove the tomato tops and hollow out the insides, creating a 1/4-inch thick shell. Chop the removed tomato flesh into fine pieces.
3. In a medium bowl, thoroughly mix the chopped tomato, diced zucchini, red onion, and red bell pepper. Stir in crumbled feta, chopped basil, olive oil, minced garlic, salt, and pepper.
4. Spoon the vegetable and feta mixture evenly into the tomato shells, packing it in gently.
5. Position the stuffed tomatoes in a baking pan or on a baking tray.
6. Bake the stuffed tomatoes in the preheated oven for 25-30 minutes, or until the tomatoes are tender and the filling is hot and bubbly.
7. Roast the stuffed tomatoes in the preheated oven for 25 to 30 minutes, or until the tomatoes soften and the filling is hot and bubbling.

Nutritional breakdown per serving:

Calories: 120 kcal, Protein: 5 grams, Carbohydrates: 12 grams, Fat: 7 grams, Saturated Fat: 2 grams, Cholesterol: 10 milligrams, Sodium: 260 milligrams, Fiber: 3 grams, and Sugar: 7 grams.

MEDITERRANEAN ROASTED VEGETABLE AND FARRO BOWLS

Total Cooking Time: 1 hour
Prep Time: 20 minutes
Servings: 4

Ingredients:

- 1 cup uncooked farro
- 1 medium eggplant, cut into 1-inch cubes
- 1 medium zucchini, cut into 1-inch cubes
- 1 red bell pepper, cut into one-inch pieces
- 1 red onion, cut into 1-inch wedges
- 3 tablespoons olive oil, divided
- 1 teaspoon dried oregano
- 1/2 teaspoon salt
- 1/4 teaspoon black pepper
- 1 cup cherry tomatoes, halved
- 1/2 cup crumbled feta cheese
- 2 tablespoons chopped fresh parsley
- 2 tablespoons lemon juice

Directions:

1. Get started by setting your oven temperature to 400°F (200°C).
2. Cook the farro according to package instructions. Drain and set aside.
3. Combine the cubed eggplant, zucchini, bell pepper, and onion in a large bowl. Drizzle with 2 tablespoons olive oil, then season with dried oregano, salt, and black pepper. Toss to coat evenly.
4. Arrange the seasoned vegetables evenly in a single layer on a large baking sheet. Roast in a preheated oven for 25 to 30 minutes, gently tossing halfway through, until tender and golden brown.
5. Toss together the cooked farro, roasted vegetables, cherry tomatoes, crumbled feta, and chopped parsley in a large bowl.
6. In a small bowl, whisk together the leftover olive oil and lemon juice until smooth. Drizzle this vinaigrette over the farro and vegetable mixture, gently tossing to coat.
7. Serve the Mediterranean Roasted Vegetable and Farro Bowls warm or at room temperature.

Nutritional breakdown per serving:

Calories: 350 kcal, Protein: 11 grams, Carbohydrates: 45 grams, Fat: 15 grams, Saturated Fat: 4 grams, Cholesterol: 15 milligrams, Sodium: 490 milligrams, Fiber: 8 grams, and Sugar: 8 grams.

GRILLED MEDITERRANEAN VEGGIE BURGERS WITH TZATZIKI SAUCE

Total Cooking Time: 45 minutes
Prep Time: 25 minutes
Servings: 4 (1 burger per serving)

Ingredients:

Veggie Burgers:

- 15 oz chickpeas, drained
- 1 cup grated zucchini, squeezed dry
- 1/2 cup crumbled feta cheese
- 1/4 cup almond flour
- 2 tablespoons chopped fresh parsley
- 1 garlic clove, minced
- 1 teaspoon ground cumin
- 1/2 teaspoon dried oregano
- 1/4 teaspoon salt
- 1/4 teaspoon black pepper

Tzatziki Sauce:

- 1 cup plain Greek yogurt
- 1/2 cup grated cucumber, squeezed dry
- 1 garlic clove, minced
- 1 tablespoon lemon juice
- 1 tablespoon chopped fresh dill
- 1/4 teaspoon salt

To Serve:

- 4 whole-wheat burger buns
- Lettuce leaves
- Sliced tomatoes
- Sliced red onion

Directions:

1. Grill or grill pan, preheated to medium-high.
2. Mash the drained and rinsed chickpeas with a fork or potato masher in a large bowl.
3. Incorporate the grated zucchini, crumbled feta, almond flour, chopped parsley, minced garlic, ground cumin, dried oregano, salt, and black pepper into the mashed chickpeas. Stir until thoroughly combined.
4. Divide the veggie burger mixture into 4 equal portions and shape them into patties, about 4 inches wide and 1/2 inch thick.
5. Grill the veggie burgers for 4-5 minutes per side, or until they are lightly charred and cooked through.
6. While the burgers are grilling, prepare the tzatziki sauce. In a small bowl, mix together the Greek yogurt, grated cucumber, minced garlic, lemon juice, chopped dill, and salt.
7. As the burgers grill, whip up a batch of tzatziki sauce. In a small bowl, blend Greek yogurt, grated cucumber, minced garlic, tangy lemon juice, fresh dill, and a pinch of salt.

Nutritional breakdown per serving:

Calories: 350 kcal, Protein: 18 grams, Carbohydrates: 42 grams, Fat: 13 grams, Saturated Fat: 5 grams, Cholesterol: 25 milligrams, Sodium: 680 milligrams, Fiber: 8 grams, and Sugar: 5 grams.

BAKED MEDITERRANEAN STUFFED ZUCCHINI BOATS

Total Cooking Time: 50 minutes
Prep Time: 20 minutes
Servings: 4 (2 stuffed zucchini halves per serving)

Ingredients:

- 4 medium zucchini, halved lengthwise
- 1 tablespoon olive oil
- 1 small onion, diced
- 2 garlic cloves, minced
- 1 cup diced tomatoes
- 1/2 cup crumbled feta cheese
- 1/4 cup chopped fresh parsley
- 2 tablespoons chopped fresh basil
- 1 teaspoon dried oregano
- 1/4 teaspoon salt
- 1/8 teaspoon black pepper
- 1/4 cup grated Parmesan cheese

Directions:

1. Get started by setting your oven temperature to 375°F (190°C).
2. Using a spoon, scoop out the flesh from the center of each zucchini half, leaving a 1/4-inch shell. Finely chop the scooped-out zucchini flesh.
3. Begin by heating olive oil in a skillet over medium heat. In the hot skillet, soften the diced onion and minced garlic by cooking for 2-3 minutes until the onion is translucent.
4. Add the chopped zucchini flesh, diced tomatoes, crumbled feta cheese, chopped parsley, chopped basil, dried oregano, salt, and black pepper. Combine ingredients thoroughly and cook for an additional 5 minutes.
5. Arrange the zucchini halves in a baking dish. Spoon the Mediterranean vegetable mixture evenly into the zucchini boats.
6. Finish the stuffed zucchini boats by sprinkling with grated Parmesan cheese.
7. Place the stuffed zucchini boats in a preheated oven and bake for 25-30 minutes, or until the zucchini softens and the filling is hot and bubbly.
8. Serve the Baked Mediterranean Stuffed Zucchini Boats warm.

Nutritional breakdown per serving:

Calories: 160 kcal, Protein: 9 grams, Carbohydrates: 12 grams, Fat: 10 grams, Saturated Fat: 4 grams, Cholesterol: 20 milligrams, Sodium: 360 milligrams, Fiber: 3 grams, and Sugar: 6 grams.

MEDITERRANEAN LENTIL AND VEGETABLE STEW

Total Cooking Time: 1 hour 10 minutes
Prep Time: 20 minutes
Servings: 6

Ingredients:

- 1 tablespoon olive oil
- 1 large onion, diced
- 3 garlic cloves, minced
- 2 carrots, peeled and diced
- 2 celery stalks, diced
- 1 red bell pepper, diced
- 1 cup brown lentils, rinsed
- 1 (14.5 oz) can diced tomatoes
- 4 cups vegetable broth
- 1 teaspoon dried oregano
- 1 teaspoon dried basil
- 1/2 teaspoon ground cumin
- 1/4 teaspoon red pepper flakes (optional)
- Salt and black pepper to taste
- 2 cups baby spinach, chopped
- 1/4 cup chopped fresh parsley

Directions:

1. Using medium heat, warm the olive oil in a large pot or Dutch oven.
2. Add the diced onion and minced garlic. Sauté for 2-3 minutes until the onion is translucent.
3. Toss in the diced carrots, celery, and red bell pepper. Gently cook the vegetables, stirring occasionally, for 5-7 minutes until slightly tender.
4. Add the rinsed brown lentils, diced tomatoes with their juice, and vegetable broth. Stir in the dried oregano, dried basil, ground cumin, and red pepper flakes (if using). Add salt and pepper to taste.
5. Bring the mixture to a boil, then reduce the heat to medium-low and let it simmer for 40-45 minutes, or until the lentils are tender.
6. Let the mixture come to a boil, then turn down the heat and simmer for 40-45 minutes, or until the lentils are tender.

7. Serve the Mediterranean Lentil and Vegetable Stew hot, garnished with additional parsley if desired.

Nutritional breakdown per serving:

Calories: 230 kcal, Protein: 13 grams, Carbohydrates: 37 grams, Fat: 4 grams, Saturated Fat: 0.5 grams, Cholesterol: 0 milligrams, Sodium: 590 milligrams, Fiber: 12 grams, and Sugar: 7 grams.

GRILLED MEDITERRANEAN VEGETABLE AND HALLOUMI SKEWERS

Total Cooking Time: 30 minutes
Prep Time: 20 minutes
Servings: 4 (2 skewers per serving)

Ingredients:

- 1 red onion, cut into 1-inch pieces
- 1 zucchini, cut into 1-inch chunks
- 1 red bell pepper, diced
- 8 ounces halloumi cheese, diced
- 2 tablespoons olive oil
- 1 tablespoon lemon juice
- 1 teaspoon dried oregano
- 1/2 teaspoon garlic powder
- 1/4 teaspoon salt
- 1/8 teaspoon black pepper
- 8 skewers (wooden or metal)

Directions:

1. In a large bowl, combine the cut red onion, zucchini, red bell pepper, and halloumi cheese.
2. Combine olive oil, lemon juice, oregano, garlic powder, salt, and pepper in a small bowl. Whisk until well blended.
3. Pour the seasoning mixture over the vegetables and halloumi, and gently toss to coat everything evenly.
4. Thread the marinated vegetables and halloumi onto the skewers, alternating the ingredients.
5. Preheat your grill or griddle to medium-high temperature.
6. Cook the skewers for 12-15 minutes, turning regularly, until the vegetables are soft and the halloumi has light grill marks.
7. Serve the skewers hot, optionally garnished with extra lemon wedges.

Nutritional breakdown per serving:

Calories: 320 kcal, Protein: 18 grams, Carbohydrates: 13 grams, Fat: 23 grams, Saturated Fat: 11 grams, Cholesterol: 45 milligrams, Sodium: 590 milligrams, Fiber: 3 grams, and Sugar: 7 grams.

BAKED MEDITERRANEAN EGGPLANT ROLLATINI WITH RICOTTA AND SPINACH

Total Cooking Time: 1 hour
Prep Time: 30 minutes
Servings: 6 (2 rollatini per serving)

Ingredients:

- 2 medium eggplants, sliced lengthwise into 1/4-inch thick slices
- 2 tablespoons olive oil, extra for brushing
- 1 onion, diced
- 3 garlic cloves, minced
- 10 oz frozen spinach, thawed & squeezed dry
- 15 ounces ricotta cheese
- 1/2 cup Parmesan, extra for topping
- 1 egg
- 1 teaspoon dried oregano
- 1/2 teaspoon salt
- 1/4 teaspoon black pepper
- 1 (24 oz) jar marinara sauce

Directions:

1. Get started by setting your oven temperature to 375°F (190°C). Cover a baking sheet with parchment paper.
2. Spread the eggplant slices evenly on the baking sheet. Brush both sides generously with olive oil.
3. Bake the eggplant slices for 15-20 minutes, flipping halfway, until softened and lightly browned. Let it cool slightly before proceeding.
4. Sauté the onion and garlic in olive oil until softened.
5. In a bowl, combine the sautéed onion and garlic, thawed and squeezed dry spinach, ricotta cheese, 1/2 cup Parmesan cheese, egg, dried oregano, salt, and black pepper. Mix well.
6. Spread about 2-3 tablespoons of the ricotta-spinach filling onto the end of each eggplant slice. Gently roll up the eggplant slice and place it seam-side down in a baking dish.
7. Pour the marinara sauce over the rolled eggplant slices, then sprinkle additional Parmesan cheese on top.

8. Bake the Eggplant Rollatini until the filling is heated through and the cheese is bubbly. This should take about 30-35 minutes.
9. Serve the Baked Mediterranean Eggplant Rollatini warm, garnished with additional Parmesan cheese, if desired.

Nutritional breakdown per serving:

Calories: 300 kcal, Protein: 17 grams, Carbohydrates: 18 grams, Fat: 19 grams, Saturated Fat: 8 grams, Cholesterol: 70 milligrams, Sodium: 780 milligrams, Fiber: 6 grams, and Sugar: 8 grams.

MEDITERRANEAN ROASTED CAULIFLOWER AND CHICKPEA SALAD

Total Cooking Time: 45 minutes
Prep Time: 15 minutes
Servings: 4

Ingredients:

- 1 head of cauliflower, cut into florets
- 15 oz chickpeas, drained
- 2 tablespoons olive oil
- 1 teaspoon ground cumin
- 1/2 teaspoon paprika
- 1/4 teaspoon cayenne pepper (optional, for a little heat)
- 1/2 teaspoon salt
- 1/4 teaspoon black pepper
- 1/2 cup crumbled feta cheese
- 1/4 cup sliced kalamata olives
- 2 tablespoons chopped fresh parsley
- 2 tablespoons lemon juice
- 1 tablespoon red wine vinegar
- 1 garlic clove, minced

Directions:

1. Get started by setting your oven temperature to 400°F (200°C). Cover a baking sheet with parchment paper.
2. Combine cauliflower florets and drained chickpeas in a large bowl. Drizzle with olive oil, cumin, paprika, cayenne pepper (if desired), salt, and black pepper. Toss to coat evenly.
3. Spread the cauliflower and chickpea mixture in a single layer on the prepared baking sheet.
4. Roast for 25-30 minutes, stirring halfway, until the cauliflower is tender and lightly browned.
5. Remove the roasted cauliflower and chickpeas from the oven and let cool slightly.
6. Combine the roasted cauliflower, chickpeas, crumbled feta, sliced olives, chopped parsley, lemon juice, red wine vinegar, and minced garlic in a large bowl. Toss gently to blend.

7. Serve the Mediterranean Roasted Cauliflower and Chickpea Salad warm or at room temperature.

Nutritional breakdown per serving:

Calories: 240 kcal, Protein: 9 grams, Carbohydrates: 22 grams, Fat: 14 grams, Saturated Fat: 4 grams, Cholesterol: 20 milligrams, Sodium: 690 milligrams, Fiber: 7 grams, and Sugar: 4 grams.

GRILLED MEDITERRANEAN VEGETABLE AND FETA STUFFED PORTOBELLO MUSHROOMS

Total Cooking Time: 45 minutes
Prep Time: 20 minutes
Servings: 4 (2 stuffed mushrooms per serving)

Ingredients:

- 8 portobello caps, stems removed, chopped
- 2 tablespoons olive oil, extra
- 1 red bell pepper, diced
- 1 zucchini, diced
- 1 red onion, diced
- 3 garlic cloves, minced
- 1 teaspoon dried oregano
- 1/2 teaspoon dried basil
- 1/4 teaspoon red pepper flakes (optional)
- 1/2 teaspoon salt
- 1/4 teaspoon black pepper
- 1 cup crumbled feta cheese
- 2 tablespoons chopped fresh parsley

Directions:

1. Grill or grill pan, preheated to medium-high.
2. Combine chopped portobello stems, bell pepper, zucchini, red onion, and garlic in a large bowl. Toss with olive oil, oregano, basil, red pepper flakes (if using), salt, and pepper.
3. Brush the portobello mushroom caps lightly with olive oil on both sides.
4. Grill the portobello mushroom caps for 3-4 minutes per side, or until they are tender and lightly charred.
5. Remove the grilled mushroom caps from the grill and place them on a work surface, gill-side up.
6. Combine crumbled feta and chopped parsley with the sautéed vegetables in the bowl. Stir to mix well.
7. Spoon the Mediterranean vegetable and feta mixture evenly into the grilled portobello mushroom caps.

8. Grill the stuffed mushrooms until the filling is hot and the cheese melts, about 3-5 minutes.
9. Serve the Grilled Mediterranean Vegetable and Feta Stuffed Portobello Mushrooms immediately, garnished with additional parsley if desired.

Nutritional breakdown per serving:

Calories: 220 kcal, Protein: 11 grams, Carbohydrates: 12 grams, Fat: 15 grams, Saturated Fat: 6 grams, Cholesterol: 30 milligrams, Sodium: 580 milligrams, Fiber: 3 grams, and Sugar: 6 grams.

BAKED MEDITERRANEAN VEGETABLE LASAGNA WITH BECHAMEL SAUCE

Total Cooking Time: 1 hour 30 minutes
Prep Time: 30 minutes
Servings: 8

Ingredients:

For the Vegetables:

- 1 eggplant, sliced into 1/2-inch thick rounds
- 2 zucchini, sliced into 1/2-inch thick rounds
- 1 red bell pepper, sliced into strips
- 1 yellow onion, thinly sliced
- 3 tablespoons olive oil
- 1 teaspoon dried oregano
- 1/2 teaspoon dried basil
- 1/4 teaspoon salt
- 1/8 teaspoon black pepper

For the Béchamel Sauce:

- 3 tablespoons unsalted butter
- 3 tablespoons all-purpose flour
- 2 cups warm milk
- 1/4 teaspoon ground nutmeg
- 1/4 teaspoon salt

For the Lasagna:

- 9 cooked lasagna noodles
- 1 cup shredded mozzarella cheese
- 1/2 cup grated Parmesan cheese

Directions:

1. Get started by setting your oven temperature to 375°F (190°C).

2. Combine eggplant, zucchini, bell pepper, and onion in a large bowl. Drizzle with olive oil, oregano, basil, salt, and pepper. Toss to coat.
3. Arrange the vegetables in a single layer on two baking sheets. Roast the vegetables for 20-25 minutes, tossing halfway through, until tender and golden. Let cool completely before proceeding.
4. Warm the butter in a saucepan over medium heat until melted. Gradually whisk in flour, cooking until the mixture is smooth and bubbly, forming a roux.
5. Incorporate the warm milk in a slow, steady stream, whisking continuously. Cook, stirring often, for approximately 5 to 7 minutes or until the sauce becomes thick. Remove from heat and blend in nutmeg and salt. Set aside to cool slightly.
6. Smoothly spread half a cup of Béchamel sauce across the base of a 9x13-inch baking pan.
7. Layer 3 cooked lasagna noodles over the sauce, then top with half of the roasted vegetables.
8. Cover the vegetables with a layer of Béchamel sauce, using about 1 cup. Sprinkle with half a cup of mozzarella and a quarter cup of Parmesan cheese.
9. Repeat the layers of noodles, vegetables, Béchamel sauce, and cheeses.
10. Finish with the remaining 3 lasagna noodles and the remaining portion of Béchamel sauce.
11. Sprinkle the top with the remaining mozzarella and Parmesan cheeses.
12. Bake the lasagna for 45-55 minutes, or until the top is golden brown and the sauce is bubbly.
13. Before serving, let the lasagna cool slightly for about 10-15 minutes.

Nutritional breakdown per serving:

Calories: 385 kcal, Protein: 18 grams, Carbohydrates: 38 grams, Fat: 18 grams, Saturated Fat: 9 grams, Cholesterol: 45 milligrams, Sodium: 580 milligrams, Fiber: 5 grams, and Sugar: 7 grams.

MEDITERRANEAN QUINOA STUFFED ACORN SQUASH

Total Cooking Time: 1 hour 15 minutes
Prep Time: 30 minutes
Servings: 4

Ingredients:

- 2 medium acorn squash halves, seeded
- 1 cup quinoa, rinsed
- 2 cups vegetable broth
- 1 tablespoon olive oil
- 1 red onion, diced
- 3 garlic cloves, minced
- 1 red bell pepper, diced
- 1 cup diced zucchini
- 1 cup diced cherry tomatoes
- 1/2 cup crumbled feta cheese
- 2 tablespoons chopped fresh parsley
- 1 teaspoon dried oregano
- 1/2 teaspoon ground cumin
- 1/4 teaspoon red pepper flakes (optional)
- Salt and black pepper to taste

Directions:

1. Get started by setting your oven temperature to 400°F (200°C).
2. Position the acorn squash halves, cut-side up, on a baking sheet. Drizzle a small amount of olive oil inside the squash halves, then season with salt and black pepper. Bake the squash until tender, about 30 to 40 minutes, or until it can be easily pierced with a fork.
3. While the squash roasts, cook the quinoa. Once the squash is in the oven, prepare the quinoa. Combine the rinsed quinoa with vegetable broth in a saucepan. Boil vigorously, then reduce heat to a simmer, cover, and cook until tender and airy, for roughly 15-20 minutes.
4. Warm a large skillet over medium heat. Add 1 tablespoon olive oil. Cook chopped onion until softened and golden, around 3-4 minutes.

5. Add the minced garlic, diced bell pepper, and diced zucchini to the skillet. Let cook for another 5-6 minutes, stirring regularly, until the vegetables are soft.
6. Return the squash to the oven and roast for another 15-20 minutes, or until the filling is heated through and the squash is easily pierced with a fork.
7. Scoop the Mediterranean quinoa mixture evenly into the baked acorn squash halves.
8. Return the stuffed squash to the oven and bake for an additional 15-20 minutes, or until the filling is heated through and the squash is fork-tender.
9. Serve the Mediterranean Quinoa Stuffed Acorn Squash warm, garnished with extra parsley if desired.

Nutritional breakdown per serving:

Calories: 335 kcal, Protein: 13 grams, Carbohydrates: 51 grams, Fat: 11 grams, Saturated Fat: 4 grams, Cholesterol: 20 milligrams, Sodium: 480 milligrams, Fiber: 9 grams, and Sugar: 8 grams.

Grilled Mediterranean Vegetable and Halloumi Skewers with Pesto Drizzle

Total Cooking Time: 35 minutes
Prep Time: 20 minutes
Servings: 4 (8 skewers)

Ingredients:

For the Skewers:

- 1 zucchini, cut into 1-inch pieces
- 1 red bell pepper, 1-inch pieces
- 1 yellow bell pepper, 1" pieces
- 1 red onion, cut into 1-inch pieces
- 8 ounces halloumi cheese, cut into 1-inch cubes
- 2 tablespoons olive oil
- 1 teaspoon dried oregano
- 1/2 teaspoon salt
- 1/4 teaspoon black pepper

For the Pesto Drizzle:

- 1 cup fresh basil leaves
- 2 garlic cloves
- 1/4 cup toasted pine nuts
- 1/4 cup grated Parmesan cheese
- 2 tablespoons olive oil
- 1 tablespoon lemon juice
- 1/4 teaspoon salt

Directions:

1. Preheat the grill to medium-high heat.
2. Combine zucchini, red and yellow bell peppers, red onion, and halloumi in a bowl. Season with olive oil, oregano, salt, and pepper. Toss to coat.
3. Thread the vegetable and halloumi pieces onto 8 metal or wooden skewers, alternating the ingredients.
4. Cook skewers on the grill for 12-15 minutes, rotating occasionally. Vegetables should be tender, and halloumi lightly browned.

5. While the skewers are grilling, prepare the pesto drizzle. Combine basil, garlic, toasted pine nuts, Parmesan, olive oil, lemon juice, and salt. Process in a food processor until a smooth pesto forms.
6. Arrange the grilled Mediterranean vegetable and halloumi skewers on a serving platter. Drizzle the pesto sauce over the top of the skewers, ensuring each skewer gets a portion of the pesto.
7. Serve the Grilled Mediterranean Vegetable and Halloumi Skewers with Pesto Drizzle immediately, while hot and fresh off the grill.

Nutritional breakdown per serving:

Calories: 270 kcal, Protein: 18 grams, Carbohydrates: 16 grams, Fat: 27 grams, Saturated Fat: 9 grams, Cholesterol: 35 milligrams, Sodium: 820 milligrams, Fiber: 3 grams, and Sugar: 7 grams.

BAKED MEDITERRANEAN FETA AND SPINACH STUFFED PORTOBELLO MUSHROOMS

Total Cooking Time: 40 minutes
Prep Time: 20 minutes
Servings: 4 (8 mushroom caps)

Ingredients:

- 4 large portobello mushroom caps, stems removed, chopped
- 2 tablespoons olive oil
- 1 shallot, finely chopped
- 3 garlic cloves, minced
- 1 cup fresh baby spinach, roughly chopped
- 1/2 cup crumbled feta cheese
- 2 tablespoons chopped fresh parsley
- 1 teaspoon dried oregano
- 1/4 teaspoon red pepper flakes (optional)
- Salt and black pepper to taste

For the Topping:

- 1/4 cup panko breadcrumbs
- 2 tablespoons grated Parmesan cheese
- 1 tablespoon olive oil

Directions:

1. Get started by setting your oven temperature to 400°F (200°C). Cover a baking sheet with parchment paper.
2. Gently clean the portobello mushroom caps with a damp paper towel. Remove and finely chop the mushroom stems.
3. Begin by heating olive oil in a skillet over medium heat. Toss in the chopped mushroom stems, shallot, and garlic. Sauté the mixture until the vegetables soften, which should take about 3 to 4 minutes.
4. Next, incorporate the chopped spinach into the skillet. Continue cooking for another 2-3 minutes, or until the spinach softens. Set the skillet aside to cool down briefly.
5. To a medium bowl, add the cooked mushroom and vegetable blend, feta cheese broken into small pieces, finely chopped parsley, dried oregano, and a pinch of red

pepper flakes if desired. Enhance the flavor by adding salt and black pepper according to your preference.
6. Carefully scoop the feta and spinach mixture into the portobello mushroom caps, dividing it evenly among the 4 caps.
7. Create a crunchy topping by combining panko, Parmesan cheese, and a drizzle of olive oil in a small bowl. Sprinkle this mixture generously over the stuffed portobello caps.
8. Place the stuffed portobello mushrooms on a baking sheet. Bake the filled portobello caps in a preheated oven for 18-22 minutes, or until they soften and the topping turns golden.
9. Serve the Baked Mediterranean Feta and Spinach Stuffed Portobello Mushrooms warm, garnished with additional parsley if desired.

Nutritional breakdown per serving:

Calories: 190 kcal, Protein: 10 grams, Carbohydrates: 13 grams, Fat: 13 grams, Saturated Fat: 5 grams, Cholesterol: 25 milligrams, Sodium: 420 milligrams, Fiber: 3 grams, and Sugar: 2 grams.

MEDITERRANEAN ROASTED VEGETABLE AND ORZO SALAD

Total Cooking Time: 50 minutes
Prep Time: 20 minutes
Servings: 6

Ingredients:

For the Roasted Vegetables:

- 1 medium zucchini, cut into 1-inch pieces
- 1 red bell pepper, diced
- 1 yellow bell pepper, diced
- 1 red onion, cut into 1-inch pieces
- 2 tablespoons olive oil
- 1 teaspoon dried oregano
- 1/2 teaspoon salt
- 1/4 teaspoon black pepper

For the Orzo Salad:

- 1 cup uncooked orzo pasta
- 1/4 cup crumbled feta cheese
- 1/4 cup pitted Kalamata olives, halved
- 2 tablespoons chopped fresh parsley
- 2 tablespoons chopped fresh basil
- 2 tablespoons lemon juice
- 1 tablespoon olive oil
- 1/2 teaspoon Dijon mustard
- 1/4 teaspoon salt
- 1/4 teaspoon black pepper

Directions:

1. Get started by setting your oven temperature to 400°F (200°C). Cover a baking sheet with parchment paper.
2. Distribute the seasoned vegetables evenly on a baking sheet. Roast for 20-25 minutes, stirring halfway, until tender and slightly browned.

3. Spread the seasoned vegetables in a single layer on the prepared baking sheet. Roast for 20-25 minutes, stirring halfway, until the vegetables are tender and lightly charred.
4. While the vegetables roast, prepare the orzo according to package directions. Drain the orzo thoroughly, then rinse with cold water until completely cooled.
5. Combine cooked, cooled orzo, roasted vegetables, crumbled feta, Kalamata olives, and chopped parsley and basil in a large bowl.
6. In a small bowl, whisk together the lemon juice, 1 tablespoon of olive oil, Dijon mustard, 1/4 teaspoon of salt, and 1/4 teaspoon of black pepper.
7. Drizzle the prepared vinaigrette over the orzo and vegetable mixture, then gently toss to coat evenly.
8. Serve the Mediterranean Roasted Vegetable and Orzo Salad chilled or at room temperature.

Nutritional breakdown per serving:

Calories: 220 kcal, Protein: 6 grams, Carbohydrates: 27 grams, Fat: 11 grams, Saturated Fat: 3 grams, Cholesterol: 10 milligrams, Sodium: 470 milligrams, Fiber: 3 grams, and Sugar: 4 grams.

GRILLED MEDITERRANEAN VEGETABLE AND HALLOUMI WRAPS WITH HUMMUS

Total Cooking Time: 30 minutes
Prep Time: 15 minutes
Servings: 4 wraps

Ingredients:

- 1 zucchini, sliced lengthwise into 1/4-inch thick strips
- 1 red bell pepper, sliced
- 1 yellow bell pepper, sliced
- 1 red onion, sliced into 1/2-inch thick rings
- 2 tablespoons olive oil, plus more for grilling
- 1 teaspoon dried oregano
- 1/2 teaspoon salt
- 1/4 teaspoon black pepper
- 8 ounces halloumi cheese, sliced into 1/4-inch thick slices
- 4 large whole wheat tortillas or wraps
- 1 cup hummus, store-bought or homemade
- 2 cups baby arugula or mixed greens

Directions:

1. Grill or grill pan, preheated to medium-high.
2. In a large bowl, mix zucchini, red and yellow bell peppers, and red onion. Drizzle with olive oil, then season with dried oregano, salt, and pepper. Toss to coat.
3. Lightly oil the grill or grill pan. Grill the vegetable slices for 2-3 minutes per side, or until they are tender and have grill marks. Transfer the grilled vegetables to a plate.
4. Grill the halloumi cheese slices for 1-2 minutes per side, or until they are lightly charred and have grill marks. Transfer the grilled halloumi to the plate with the vegetables.
5. Spread a quarter cup of hummus on each tortilla or wrap, leaving a one-inch border.
6. Arrange the grilled vegetables and halloumi cheese slices in the center of the tortillas. Top with the baby arugula or mixed greens.
7. Enclose the filling by folding the bottom of the tortilla over it, tucking in the sides, and rolling the wrap tightly.
8. Serve the Grilled Mediterranean Vegetable and Halloumi Wraps with Hummus immediately.

Nutritional breakdown per serving :

Calories: 410 kcal, Protein: 17 grams, Carbohydrates: 40 grams, Fat: 22 grams, Saturated Fat: 8 grams, Cholesterol: 35 milligrams, Sodium: 920 milligrams, Fiber: 7 grams, and Sugar: 5 grams.

BAKED MEDITERRANEAN STUFFED EGGPLANT WITH TOMATO-BASIL SAUCE

Total Cooking Time: 1 hour 15 minutes
Prep Time: 30 minutes
Servings: 4

Ingredients:

For the Stuffed Eggplant:

- 2 medium eggplants, halved lengthwise
- 2 tablespoons olive oil, plus more for brushing
- 1 cup cooked quinoa
- 1/2 cup chopped fresh parsley
- 1/4 cup crumbled feta cheese
- 2 cloves garlic, minced
- 1 teaspoon dried oregano
- 1/4 teaspoon salt
- 1/4 teaspoon black pepper

For the Tomato-Basil Sauce:

- 1 tablespoon olive oil
- 1 small onion, diced
- 3 cloves garlic, minced
- 1 (14.5 oz) can diced tomatoes
- 1/4 cup chopped fresh basil
- 1 teaspoon dried oregano
- 1/4 teaspoon salt
- 1/4 teaspoon black pepper

Directions:

1. Get started by setting your oven temperature to 400°F (200°C). Cover a baking sheet with parchment paper.
2. Cut eggplants in half lengthwise. Scoop out the flesh, creating a half-inch thick shell. Chop the removed eggplant into small pieces.

3. Place the eggplant halves, cut-side up, on the prepared baking sheet. Brush the eggplant shells with olive oil. Roast the eggplant halves until tender and the flesh is easily scooped out, about 20-25 minutes.
4. In a medium bowl, thoroughly combine diced eggplant, cooked quinoa, chopped parsley, crumbled feta, minced garlic, dried oregano, salt, and pepper.
5. Spoon the quinoa-eggplant mixture evenly into the baked eggplant halves.
6. Return the stuffed eggplant halves to the oven and bake for an additional 20-25 minutes, or until the filling is heated through and the eggplant is very tender.
7. While the eggplant is baking, prepare the Tomato-Basil Sauce. Heat a tablespoon of olive oil in a medium saucepan over medium heat. Add the diced onion and garlic, and sauté for 2-3 minutes, or until the onion is translucent.
8. Elevate the sauce with a vibrant blend of diced tomatoes, fresh basil, dried oregano, salt, and pepper. Gently simmer on low heat for 10-15 minutes, stirring occasionally, until the sauce thickens slightly.
9. Serve the Baked Mediterranean Stuffed Eggplant with the Tomato-Basil Sauce spooned over the top.

Nutritional breakdown per serving:

Calories: 250 kcal, Protein: 9 grams, Carbohydrates: 29 grams, Fat: 12 grams, Saturated Fat: 3 grams, Cholesterol: 15 milligrams, Sodium: 430 milligrams, Fiber: 8 grams, and Sugar: 10 grams.

MEDITERRANEAN ROASTED VEGETABLE AND FETA QUINOA BOWLS

Total Cooking Time: 45 minutes
Prep Time: 20 minutes
Servings: 4 bowls

Ingredients:

- 1 cup uncooked quinoa, rinsed
- 2 cups vegetable or chicken broth
- 1 medium zucchini, cut into 1-inch pieces
- 1 red bell pepper, diced
- 1 yellow bell pepper, diced
- 1 red onion, cut into 1-inch wedges
- 1 pint cherry tomatoes, halved
- 3 tablespoons olive oil, divided
- 1 teaspoon dried oregano
- 1/2 teaspoon salt
- 1/4 teaspoon black pepper
- 1/2 cup crumbled feta cheese
- 1/4 cup pitted Kalamata olives, halved
- 2 tablespoons chopped fresh parsley
- 1 tablespoon lemon juice

Directions:

1. Get started by setting your oven temperature to 400°F (200°C). Cover a baking sheet with parchment paper.
2. Combine quinoa and broth in a medium-sized saucepan. Once the mixture boils, lower the heat, cover the pan, and simmer until the quinoa is tender and all the liquid is absorbed. This typically takes 15-20 minutes. Fluff with a fork before serving.
3. Combine zucchini, red and yellow bell peppers, and red onion in a large bowl. Coat the vegetables generously with olive oil, then season with dried oregano, salt, and pepper. Toss gently to combine.
4. Distribute the seasoned vegetables evenly on the baking sheet. Roast for 20-25 minutes, or until tender and slightly caramelized.

5. Toss together cooked quinoa, roasted vegetables, cherry tomatoes, feta cheese, Kalamata olives, parsley, and lemon juice in a large bowl. Gently drizzle with the remaining olive oil and mix lightly.
6. Divide the Mediterranean Roasted Vegetable and Feta Quinoa mixture evenly among 4 serving bowls.

Nutritional breakdown per serving:

Calories: 380 kcal, Protein: 13 grams, Carbohydrates: 42 grams, Fat: 18 grams, Saturated Fat: 5 grams, Cholesterol: 20 milligrams, Sodium: 750 milligrams, Fiber: 7 grams, and Sugar: 7 grams.

GRILLED MEDITERRANEAN VEGETABLE AND CHICKPEA SKEWERS WITH TAHINI DRIZZLE

Total Cooking Time: 35 minutes
Prep Time: 20 minutes
Servings: 4 (3 skewers per serving)

Ingredients:

- 15 oz chickpeas, drained
- 1 zucchini, cut into 1-inch pieces
- 1 red bell pepper, diced
- 1 yellow bell pepper, diced
- 1 red onion, cut into 1-inch pieces
- 8 oz button mushrooms, halved
- 2 tablespoons olive oil
- 1 teaspoon dried oregano
- 1/2 teaspoon salt
- 1/4 teaspoon black pepper

For the Tahini Drizzle:

- 1/4 cup tahini
- 2 tablespoons water
- 1 tablespoon lemon juice
- 1 clove garlic, minced
- 1/4 teaspoon salt

Directions:

1. Grill or grill pan, preheated to medium-high.
2. Toss chickpeas, diced zucchini, red and yellow bell peppers, red onion, and sliced mushrooms in a large bowl. Combine with olive oil, oregano, salt, and pepper.
3. Thread the seasoned vegetables and chickpeas onto 12 metal or wooden skewers, dividing the ingredients evenly.
4. Cook the skewers on the grill for 12-15 minutes, turning frequently, until tender and lightly browned.
5. While the skewers cook, prepare the tahini sauce. Combine tahini, water, lemon juice, garlic, and salt in a bowl. Whisk until smooth and creamy.

6. Arrange the grilled Mediterranean Vegetable and Chickpea Skewers on a serving platter. Drizzle the Tahini Drizzle over the top of the skewers, ensuring each skewer gets a portion of the sauce.
7. Serve the Grilled Mediterranean Vegetable and Chickpea Skewers with Tahini Drizzle immediately.

Nutritional breakdown per serving:

Calories: 320 kcal, Protein: 12 grams, Carbohydrates: 35 grams, Fat: 16 grams, Saturated Fat: 2 grams, Cholesterol: 0 milligrams, Sodium: 550 milligrams, Fiber: 9 grams, and Sugar: 8 grams.

BAKED MEDITERRANEAN ZUCCHINI BOATS WITH QUINOA AND FETA

Total Cooking Time: 45 minutes
Prep Time: 20 minutes
Servings: 4 (2 zucchini boats per serving)

Ingredients:

- 4 medium-sized zucchini, halved lengthwise
- 1 cup cooked quinoa
- 1 (15 oz) can diced tomatoes
- 1/2 cup crumbled feta cheese
- 1/4 cup chopped fresh parsley
- 2 cloves garlic, minced
- 1 teaspoon dried oregano
- 1/2 teaspoon salt
- 1/4 teaspoon black pepper
- 2 tablespoons olive oil

Directions:

1. Get started by setting your oven temperature to 400°F (200°C). Cover a baking sheet with parchment paper.
2. Scoop out the flesh from the center of each zucchini half, leaving a 1/4-inch border to create "boats." Finely chop the scooped-out zucchini flesh.
3. Combine chopped zucchini, cooked quinoa, diced tomatoes, crumbled feta, parsley, garlic, dried oregano, salt, and pepper in a large bowl. Mix well.
4. Position the zucchini boats on the prepared baking sheet. Fill the zucchini boats evenly with the quinoa and vegetable mixture.
5. Drizzle the tops of the filled zucchini boats with the olive oil.
6. Roast for 25-30 minutes, or until the zucchini softens and the filling is hot and bubbly.
7. Remove the baked zucchini boats from the oven and serve immediately.

Nutritional breakdown per serving:

Calories: 220 kcal, Protein: 10 grams, Carbohydrates: 20 grams, Fat: 12 grams, Saturated Fat: 4 grams, Cholesterol: 15 milligrams, Sodium: 480 milligrams, Fiber: 4 grams, and Sugar: 6 grams.

MEDITERRANEAN ROASTED CAULIFLOWER AND LENTIL SALAD

Total Cooking Time: 45 minutes
Prep Time: 20 minutes
Servings: 4

Ingredients:

- 1 head cauliflower, cut into small pieces
- 2 tablespoons olive oil
- 1 teaspoon dried oregano
- 1/2 teaspoon salt
- 1/4 teaspoon black pepper
- 1 cup cooked lentils
- 1 cup cherry tomatoes, halved
- 1/2 cup crumbled feta cheese
- 1/4 cup pitted kalamata olives, sliced
- 2 tablespoons chopped fresh parsley
- 2 tablespoons lemon juice
- 1 tablespoon red wine vinegar
- 1 clove garlic, minced

Directions:

1. Get started by setting your oven temperature to 400°F (200°C). Cover a baking sheet with parchment paper.
2. Combine cauliflower florets, olive oil, dried oregano, salt, and pepper in a large bowl. Toss to coat.
3. Distribute the seasoned cauliflower evenly on the baking sheet.
4. Roast the cauliflower until tender and golden brown, about 20-25 minutes.
5. Let the roasted cauliflower cool slightly after removing it from the oven.
6. Combine roasted cauliflower, cooked lentils, cherry tomatoes, crumbled feta, kalamata olives, and fresh parsley in a large bowl.
7. Combine lemon juice, red wine vinegar, and minced garlic in a small bowl. Whisk until blended. Combine the salad and dressing, tossing gently to coat.
8. Serve the Mediterranean Roasted Cauliflower and Lentil Salad at room temperature or chilled.

Nutritional breakdown per serving:

Calories: 250 kcal, Protein: 12 grams, Carbohydrates: 25 grams, Fat: 12 grams, Saturated Fat: 3 grams, Cholesterol: 10 milligrams, Sodium: 640 milligrams, Fiber: 8 grams, and Sugar: 6 grams.

CHAPTER 5
FRESH AND FLAVORFUL FISH DISHES

GRILLED MEDITERRANEAN SEA BREAM WITH LEMON-HERB MARINADE

Total Time: 30 minutes
Prep Time: 15 minutes
Servings: 4

Ingredients:

- 4 (6 oz) sea bream fillets, skin-on
- 3 tbsp olive oil
- 2 tbsp freshly squeezed lemon juice
- 3 garlic cloves, minced
- 2 tsp dried oregano
- 1 tsp grated lemon zest
- 1 tsp honey
- 1/2 tsp salt
- 1/4 tsp black pepper

Instructions:

1. In a shallow baking dish or resealable bag, combine olive oil, lemon juice, garlic, oregano, grated lemon zest, honey, salt, and pepper to create a marinade. Add the sea bream fillets and ensure they are evenly coated with the marinade. Refrigerate the marinating fish for 30 to 60 minutes, covered.
2. Get your grill or grill pan ready by preheating it to medium-high.
3. Remove the fillets from the marinade and place them skin-side down on the hot grill. Cook the fish for 4-5 minutes per side, or until it flakes easily with a fork and the skin is crispy.
4. Transfer the grilled sea bream fillets to a serving platter. Serve immediately, garnished with fresh lemon wedges if desired.

Nutritional breakdown per serving:

Calories: 270 kcal, Protein: 27 grams, Carbohydrates: 4 grams, Fat: 15 grams, Saturated Fat: 2 grams, Cholesterol: 80 milligrams, Sodium: 420 milligrams, Fiber: 0 grams, and Sugar: 2 grams.

BAKED COD WITH TOMATO, OLIVE, AND CAPER TOPPING

Total Time: 35 minutes
Prep Time: 15 minutes
Servings: 4

Ingredients:

- 4 (6 oz) cod fillets
- 2 tbsp olive oil
- 1 cup diced tomatoes
- 2 tablespoons sliced black olives
- 2 tbsp capers, rinsed and drained
- 2 garlic cloves, minced
- 1 tbsp chopped fresh parsley
- 1 tsp honey
- 1/2 tsp dried oregano
- 1/4 tsp red pepper flakes (optional)
- Salt and black pepper to taste

Instructions:

1. Begin by adjusting the oven temperature to 400°F (200°C).
2. Grab a medium-sized bowl and add the following ingredients: diced tomatoes, sliced olives, capers, garlic, parsley, honey, dried oregano, and red pepper flakes (if you'd like to include them). Season to taste with salt and pepper.
3. Put the cod fillets in a baking dish and evenly drizzle them with olive oil, making certain the fillets are thoroughly coated.
4. Spoon the tomato-olive-caper topping over the cod fillets, spreading it out evenly.
5. Transfer the cod to the pre-heated oven and let it bake for 15-20 minutes, or until the fish appears opaque and can be readily flaked with a fork.
6. Serve the baked cod immediately, garnished with additional parsley if desired.

Nutritional breakdown per serving:

Calories: 265 kcal, Protein: 32 grams, Carbohydrates: 8 grams, Fat: 11 grams, Saturated Fat: 2 grams, Cholesterol: 70 milligrams, Sodium: 580 milligrams, Fiber: 2 grams, and Sugar: 3 grams.

SAUTÉED SHRIMP AND ZUCCHINI NOODLE STIR-FRY

Total Time: 25 minutes
Prep Time: 15 minutes
Servings: 4

Ingredients:

- 1 lb peeled and deveined shrimp
- 2 tbsp olive oil
- 3 garlic cloves, minced
- 1 tsp grated ginger
- 1/4 cup low-sodium soy sauce
- 2 tbsp rice vinegar
- 1 tbsp honey
- 1 tsp sesame oil
- 1/4 tsp red pepper flakes (optional)
- 3 medium zucchini, spiralized or julienned into noodles
- 2 cups sliced mushrooms
- 1 cup thinly sliced bell pepper
- 2 green onions, sliced
- Salt and black pepper to taste

Instructions:

1. Whisk together soy sauce, rice vinegar, honey, sesame oil, and red pepper flakes (if desired) in a small bowl.
2. To a large skillet or wok heated over medium-high heat, add olive oil. When the oil was hot, add the shrimp and cook until they were cooked through and had a pink color, stirring occasionally. Take the shrimp out of the pan and keep them aside.
3. Sauté the garlic and ginger in the skillet for 1 minute, until they become fragrant.
4. Add the zucchini noodles, mushrooms, and bell pepper to the skillet. Sauté for 3-4 minutes, stirring frequently, until the vegetables are tender-crisp.
5. Add the shrimp back to the skillet and pour the soy sauce mixture over it. Toss everything together and cook for another 2-3 minutes until the sauce thickens slightly.
6. Turn off the heat and incorporate the sliced green onions into the skillet by stirring. Season to taste with salt and pepper.

7. Serve the sautéed shrimp and zucchini noodle stir-fry immediately, garnished with additional green onions if desired.

Nutritional breakdown per serving:

Calories: 280 kcal, Protein: 26 grams, Carbohydrates: 16 grams, Fat: 12 grams, Saturated Fat: 2 grams, Cholesterol: 190 milligrams, Sodium: 680 milligrams, Fiber: 3 grams, and Sugar: 7 grams.

POACHED SALMON WITH DILL YOGURT SAUCE

Total Time: 30 minutes
Prep Time: 10 minutes
Servings: 4

Ingredients:

Poached Salmon:

- 4 (6 oz) salmon fillets
- 4 cups water
- 2 tablespoons lemon juice
- 1 teaspoon salt
- 1/2 teaspoon black pepper

Dill Yogurt Sauce:

- 1 cup plain Greek yogurt
- 2 tablespoons chopped fresh dill
- 1 tablespoon lemon juice
- 1 garlic clove, minced
- 1/4 teaspoon salt
- 1/8 teaspoon black pepper

Instructions:

Poached Salmon:

1. In a large skillet or saucepan, combine the water, lemon juice, salt, and black pepper. Simmer the mixture gently over medium heat.

2. Gently add the salmon fillets to the simmering liquid, making sure they are submerged. Poach the salmon until it is opaque and flakes easily with a fork, which should take about 8-10 minutes.

3. Using a slotted spoon, transfer the poached salmon fillets to a plate. Cover and keep warm.

Dill Yogurt Sauce:

    4. In a small bowl, combine the Greek yogurt, chopped dill, lemon juice, garlic, salt, and black pepper. Stir until well mixed.

To Serve:

    5. Place a poached salmon fillet on each serving plate.

    6. Spoon a generous amount of the dill yogurt sauce over the top of the salmon.

    7. Serve the poached salmon with the dill yogurt sauce immediately.

Nutritional breakdown per serving:

Calories: 295 kcal, Protein: 39 grams, Carbohydrates: 5 grams, Fat: 13 grams, Saturated Fat: 3 grams, Cholesterol: 90 milligrams, Sodium: 625 milligrams, Fiber: 0 grams, and Sugar: 3 grams.

MEDITERRANEAN TUNA AND WHITE BEAN SALAD

Total Time: 20 minutes
Prep Time: 15 minutes
Servings: 4

Ingredients:

- 2 (5 oz) cans of tuna, drained
- 1 can (15 oz) white beans, rinsed and drained
- 1 cup halved cherry tomatoes
- 2 tablespoons pitted and halved kalamata olives
- 1/4 cup crumbled feta cheese
- 2 tablespoons chopped fresh parsley
- 2 tablespoons olive oil
- 1 tablespoon red wine vinegar
- 1 tablespoon lemon juice
- 1 garlic clove, minced
- 1/2 teaspoon dried oregano
- 1/4 teaspoon salt
- 1/8 teaspoon black pepper

Instructions:

1. In a large bowl, mix together the drained tuna, rinsed and drained white beans, halved cherry tomatoes, halved kalamata olives, crumbled feta cheese, and chopped fresh parsley.
2. Toss together olive oil, red wine vinegar, lemon juice, minced garlic, dried oregano, salt, and black pepper in a small bowl. Whisk until well combined.
3. Toss the tuna and bean mixture with the dressing, being careful not to overmix.
4. Serve the Mediterranean Tuna and White Bean Salad chilled or at room temperature.

Nutritional breakdown per serving:

Calories: 270 kcal, Protein: 22 grams, Carbohydrates: 17 grams, Fat: 13 grams, Saturated Fat: 3 grams, Cholesterol: 25 milligrams, Sodium: 590 milligrams, Fiber: 5 grams, and Sugar: 2 grams.

ROASTED TROUT WITH ROASTED RED PEPPER SAUCE

Total Time: 45 minutes
Prep Time: 20 minutes
Servings: 4

Ingredients:

Roasted Trout:

- 4 (6 oz) trout fillets
- 2 tablespoons olive oil
- 1 teaspoon garlic powder
- 1 teaspoon paprika
- 1/2 teaspoon salt
- 1/4 teaspoon black pepper

Roasted Red Pepper Sauce:

- 2 red bell peppers, roasted and peeled
- 1/4 cup plain Greek yogurt
- 2 tablespoons lemon juice
- 2 garlic cloves, minced
- 1/4 teaspoon salt
- 1/8 teaspoon black pepper

Instructions:

Roasted Trout:

1. Begin by adjusting the oven temperature to 400°F (200°C).

2. Lay the trout fillets, patted dry with paper towels, on a parchment paper-lined baking sheet.

3. Drizzle the trout fillets with olive oil and sprinkle with garlic powder, paprika, salt, and black pepper. Rub the seasoning evenly over the fillets.

4. Roast the trout until it flakes easily with a fork, which should take about 12-15 minutes in the preheated oven.

Roasted Red Pepper Sauce:

5. Grill the red bell peppers over an open flame or under the broiler, rotating them regularly until the skin is charred. Steam the roasted peppers by placing them in a bowl, covering it with plastic wrap, and letting them sit for 10-15 minutes.

6. Remove the seeds and stems from the roasted peppers, then peel off the skin.

7. Using a food processor or blender, mix together the roasted red peppers, Greek yogurt, lemon juice, minced garlic, salt, and black pepper. Blend until you reach a perfectly smooth texture.

To Serve:

8. Place a roasted trout fillet on each serving plate.

9. Spoon a generous amount of the roasted red pepper sauce over the top of the trout.

10. Serve the roasted trout with the roasted red pepper sauce immediately.

Nutritional breakdown per serving:

Calories: 320 kcal, Protein: 36 grams, Carbohydrates: 9 grams, Fat: 15 grams, Saturated Fat: 3 grams, Cholesterol: 100 milligrams, Sodium: 600 milligrams, Fiber: 2 grams, and Sugar: 4 grams.

BAKED HALIBUT WITH FENNEL AND ORANGE SALAD

Total Time: 45 minutes
Prep Time: 25 minutes
Servings: 4

Ingredients:

Baked Halibut:

- 4 (6 oz) halibut fillets
- 2 tablespoons olive oil
- 1 teaspoon grated lemon zest
- 1 teaspoon dried thyme
- 1/2 teaspoon salt
- 1/4 teaspoon black pepper

Fennel and Orange Salad:

- 1 bulb fennel, thinly sliced (about 2 cups)
- 2 oranges, peeled and segmented
- 1/4 cup thinly sliced red onion
- 2 tablespoons olive oil
- 1 tablespoon balsamic vinegar
- 1 tablespoon chopped fresh parsley
- 1/4 teaspoon salt
- 1/8 teaspoon black pepper

Instructions:

Baked Halibut:

1. Begin by adjusting the oven temperature to 400°F (200°C).

2. Arrange the halibut fillets in a baking dish. Pour olive oil over them and season with lemon zest, dried thyme, salt, and black pepper. Rub the seasoning evenly over the fillets.

3. Bake the halibut in the preheated oven for 15-18 minutes, or until it is cooked through and flakes easily with a fork.

Fennel and Orange Salad:

4. Mix together the thinly sliced fennel, orange segments, and sliced red onion in a large bowl.

5. Combine olive oil, balsamic vinegar, chopped parsley, salt, and black pepper in a small bowl and whisk until well combined.

6. Combine the fennel and orange mixture with the dressing by gently tossing them together.

To Serve:

7. Place a baked halibut fillet on each serving plate.

8. Spoon the fennel and orange salad alongside the baked halibut.

9. Serve the baked halibut with the fennel and orange salad immediately.

Nutritional breakdown per serving:

Calories: 350 kcal, Protein: 38 grams, Carbohydrates: 17 grams, Fat: 16 grams, Saturated Fat: 2 grams, Cholesterol: 80 milligrams, Sodium: 550 milligrams, Fiber: 4 grams, and Sugar: 9 grams.

GRILLED SWORDFISH SKEWERS WITH PINEAPPLE SALSA

Total Time: 40 minutes
Prep Time: 20 minutes
Servings: 4

Ingredients:

Swordfish Skewers:

- 1 lb swordfish, cut into 1-inch cubes
- 2 tablespoons olive oil
- 1 teaspoon ground cumin
- 1 teaspoon chili powder
- 1/2 teaspoon salt
- 1/4 teaspoon black pepper

Pineapple Salsa:

- 1 cup diced fresh pineapple
- 1/2 cup diced red onion
- 1/4 cup chopped fresh cilantro
- 2 tablespoons lime juice
- 1 jalapeño pepper, seeded and finely chopped (optional)
- 1/4 teaspoon salt

Instructions:

Swordfish Skewers:

1. Grill or grill pan, preheated to medium-high.

2. In a medium bowl, combine the swordfish cubes, olive oil, ground cumin, chili powder, salt, and black pepper. Toss to coat the swordfish evenly.

3. Thread the seasoned swordfish cubes onto skewers, leaving a little space between each piece.

4. Cook the swordfish skewers on the grill for 2-3 minutes per side, or until they are cooked through and flake easily with a fork.

Pineapple Salsa:

5. Mix together the diced pineapple, red onion, chopped cilantro, lime juice, and jalapeño (if using) in a medium bowl.

6. Season the salsa with salt and stir to combine.

To Serve:

7. Place the grilled swordfish skewers on a serving platter.

8. Top the swordfish skewers with the pineapple salsa.

9. Serve the Grilled Swordfish Skewers with Pineapple Salsa immediately.

Nutritional breakdown per serving:

Calories: 280 kcal, Protein: 28 grams, Carbohydrates: 16 grams, Fat: 12 grams, Saturated Fat: 2 grams, Cholesterol: 75 milligrams, Sodium: 480 milligrams, Fiber: 2 grams, and Sugar: 10 grams.

MEDITERRANEAN MUSSELS IN WHITE WINE BROTH

Total Time: 30 minutes
Prep Time: 15 minutes
Servings: 4

Ingredients:

- 2 lbs mussels, scrubbed and debearded
- 2 tablespoons olive oil
- 3 garlic cloves, minced
- 1 shallot, thinly sliced
- 1 cup dry white wine
- 1 cup low-sodium chicken or vegetable broth
- 1 (14.5 oz) can diced tomatoes
- 1 teaspoon dried oregano
- 1/4 teaspoon red pepper flakes (optional)
- 1/4 cup chopped fresh parsley
- 1 baguette, sliced, for serving

Instructions:

1. To a large pot or Dutch oven heated over medium heat, add olive oil. Once the oil is hot, introduce the minced garlic and sliced shallot. Cook the minced garlic and sliced shallot for 2-3 minutes, stirring occasionally, until they become fragrant and softened.
2. Combine white wine and chicken or vegetable broth in the pot. Add the diced tomatoes (with their juices), dried oregano, and red pepper flakes (if using). Stir to combine.
3. Heat the mixture until it simmers. Then, add the mussels, which have been scrubbed and debearded, to the pot. Close the pot and cook for 5-7 minutes, or until the mussels open.
4. Remove the pot from the heat source and throw away any mussels that did not open.
5. Add the chopped fresh parsley to the pot and season with salt and pepper to your liking.
6. Serve the Mediterranean Mussels in White Wine Broth immediately, with the sliced baguette on the side for dipping in the flavorful broth.

Nutritional breakdown per serving:

Calories: 320 kcal, Protein: 25 grams, Carbohydrates: 28 grams, Fat: 10 grams, Saturated Fat: 1.5 grams, Cholesterol: 80 milligrams, Sodium: 820 milligrams, Fiber: 3 grams, and Sugar: 4 grams.

BAKED STUFFED CALAMARI WITH HERBED BREADCRUMBS

Total Time: 60 minutes
Prep Time: 30 minutes
Servings: 4

Ingredients:

Calamari Filling:

- 1 lb fresh calamari, cleaned and tentacles chopped
- 1/2 cup finely chopped onion
- 2 garlic cloves, minced
- 1/4 cup chopped fresh parsley
- 1 tablespoon lemon juice
- 1/2 teaspoon dried oregano
- 1/4 teaspoon red pepper flakes (optional)
- Salt and black pepper to taste

Herbed Breadcrumb Topping:

- 1 cup panko breadcrumbs
- 1/4 cup grated Parmesan cheese
- 2 tablespoons chopped fresh parsley
- 1 tablespoon chopped fresh basil
- 2 garlic cloves, minced
- 2 tablespoons olive oil
- Salt and black pepper to taste

Instructions:

1. Begin by adjusting the oven temperature to 375°F (190°C).
2. In a medium bowl, combine all the calamari filling ingredients: chopped calamari, onion, garlic, parsley, lemon juice, oregano, red pepper flakes (if using), and season with salt and black pepper. Mix well and set aside.
3. In another bowl, prepare the herbed breadcrumb topping by mixing together the panko breadcrumbs, Parmesan cheese, chopped parsley, chopped basil, minced garlic, olive oil, and season with salt and black pepper. Mix until well combined.

4. Carefully stuff the calamari bodies with the calamari filling mixture, being careful not to overstuff.
5. Arrange the stuffed calamari in a baking dish or on a parchment-lined baking sheet. Sprinkle the herbed breadcrumb topping evenly over the stuffed calamari.
6. Bake the stuffed calamari for 25-30 minutes, or until the breadcrumbs are golden brown and the calamari is cooked through.
7. Enjoy the Baked Stuffed Calamari with Herbed Breadcrumbs warm, topped with extra chopped parsley if you like.

Nutritional breakdown per serving:

Calories: 260 kcal, Protein: 22 grams, Carbohydrates: 20 grams, Fat: 9 grams, Saturated Fat: 2 grams, Cholesterol: 320 milligrams, Sodium: 620 milligrams, Fiber: 1 grams, and Sugar: 2 grams.

SEARED SCALLOPS WITH ASPARAGUS AND LEMON VINAIGRETTE

Total Time: 25 minutes
Prep Time: 15 minutes
Servings: 4

Ingredients:

Lemon Vinaigrette:

- 2 tablespoons lemon juice
- 1 tablespoon white wine vinegar
- 1 teaspoon Dijon mustard
- 1/4 cup olive oil
- Salt and black pepper to taste

Scallops and Asparagus:

- 1 lb fresh sea scallops, patted dry
- 1 lb asparagus, trimmed and cut into 1-inch pieces
- 1 tablespoon olive oil
- Salt and black pepper to taste

Instructions:

Lemon Vinaigrette:

1. Toss together lemon juice, white wine vinegar, and Dijon mustard in a small bowl. Whisk until well combined.

2. Gradually add the olive oil to the vinaigrette, whisking continuously until it is emulsified.

3. Add salt and pepper, then set aside.

Scallops and Asparagus:

4. Heat a large skillet over medium-high heat. Add the olive oil.

5. Season the scallops with salt and pepper after patting them dry with paper towels.

6. Gently add the scallops to the hot skillet and cook them for 2-3 minutes per side, or until they develop a golden-brown crust. Transfer the seared scallops to a plate.

7. In the same skillet, add the asparagus pieces and sauté for 3-4 minutes, or until they are tender-crisp.

8. Return the seared scallops to the skillet with the asparagus and toss gently to combine.

9. Drizzle the prepared lemon vinaigrette over the scallops and asparagus, and serve immediately.

Nutritional breakdown per serving:

Calories: 230 kcal, Protein: 17 grams, Carbohydrates: 10 grams, Fat: 15 grams, Saturated Fat: 2 grams, Cholesterol: 35 milligrams, Sodium: 450 milligrams, Fiber: 2 grams, and Sugar: 2 grams.

MEDITERRANEAN SEAFOOD STEW WITH TOMATOES AND HERBS

Total Time: 45 minutes
Prep Time: 20 minutes
Servings: 4

Ingredients:

- 1 lb mixed seafood (such as shrimp, mussels, clams, and cod), cleaned and prepared
- 2 tablespoons olive oil
- 1 onion, diced
- 3 garlic cloves, minced
- 1 teaspoon dried oregano
- 1 teaspoon dried thyme
- 1 (14.5 oz) can diced tomatoes
- 1 cup fish or vegetable broth
- 1/2 cup dry white wine
- 1 lemon, zested and juiced
- 1/4 cup chopped fresh parsley
- 1/4 cup chopped fresh basil
- Salt and black pepper to taste

Instructions:

1. Introduce olive oil into a large Dutch oven or heavy pot that has been heated to medium.
2. Add the diced onion and sauté for 3-4 minutes, until translucent.
3. Combine minced garlic, dried oregano, and dried thyme in the skillet and cook until fragrant. This should take about 1 minute.
4. Pour in the diced tomatoes, fish or vegetable broth, and dry white wine. Bring the mixture to a simmer.
5. Add the mixed seafood (shrimp, mussels, clams, and cod) to the pot. Cover and simmer for 10-12 minutes, or until the seafood is cooked through and the mussels and clams have opened up.
6. Incorporate the lemon zest, lemon juice, chopped parsley, and chopped basil into the pot. Add salt and pepper as desired.
7. Serve the Mediterranean Seafood Stew hot, garnished with additional fresh herbs if desired. Enjoy with crusty bread for dipping in the flavorful broth.

Nutritional breakdown per serving:

Calories: 290 kcal, Protein: 30 grams, Carbohydrates: 14 grams, Fat: 10 grams, Saturated Fat: 2 grams, Cholesterol: 150 milligrams, Sodium: 820 milligrams, Fiber: 3 grams, and Sugar: 5 grams.

GRILLED WHOLE BRANZINO WITH LEMON AND HERBS

Total Time: 35 minutes
Prep Time: 20 minutes
Servings: 2

Ingredients:

- 2 whole branzino fish, cleaned and scaled (about 1-1.5 lbs each)
- 2 tablespoons olive oil, with extra for greasing the grill
- 2 lemons, zested and juiced
- 3 garlic cloves, minced
- 1 tablespoon chopped fresh parsley
- 1 tablespoon chopped fresh oregano
- 1 tablespoon chopped fresh thyme
- Salt and black pepper to taste

Instructions:

1. Pat the whole branzino fish dry with paper towels. Make 3-4 shallow diagonal cuts on each side of the fish.
2. Toss together olive oil, lemon zest, lemon juice, minced garlic, chopped parsley, oregano, and thyme in a small bowl. Whisk until well combined. Season with salt and pepper.
3. Turn on the grill to medium-high heat and lightly grease the grates.
4. Place the whole branzino fish on the preheated grill grates. Cook for 4-5 minutes per side, or until the fish is opaque and flakes easily with a fork.
5. Carefully transfer the grilled branzino to a serving platter. Drizzle the prepared lemon and herb mixture over the top of the fish.
6. Serve the Grilled Whole Branzino with Lemon and Herbs immediately, garnished with additional fresh herbs if desired. Enjoy with roasted vegetables or a fresh salad.

Nutritional breakdown per serving:

Calories: 360 kcal, Protein: 46 grams, Carbohydrates: 5 grams, Fat: 19 grams, Saturated Fat: 3 grams, Cholesterol: 120 milligrams, Sodium: 380 milligrams, Fiber: 1 grams, and Sugar: 1 grams.

BAKED SALMON CAKES WITH DILL AND LEMON

Total Time: 45 minutes
Prep Time: 20 minutes
Servings: 4 (4 cakes per serving)

Ingredients:

- 1 lb boneless, skinless salmon fillets, cooked and flaked
- 1 cup panko breadcrumbs
- 1/4 cup finely chopped dill
- 2 tablespoons lemon juice
- 1 tablespoon lemon zest
- 1 egg, lightly beaten
- 2 tablespoons mayonnaise
- 1 tablespoon Dijon mustard
- 1/4 cup all-purpose flour
- 2 tablespoons olive oil
- Salt and black pepper to taste

For the Dill Lemon Sauce:

- 1/2 cup plain Greek yogurt
- 2 tablespoons lemon juice
- 1 tablespoon chopped fresh dill
- 1 garlic clove, minced
- Salt and black pepper to taste

Instructions:

1. Begin by adjusting the oven temperature to 400°F (200°C). Cover a baking sheet with parchment paper.
2. In a large bowl, gently mix together the cooked and flaked salmon, panko breadcrumbs, chopped dill, lemon juice, lemon zest, beaten egg, mayonnaise, and Dijon mustard. Add salt and pepper to taste.
3. Create 16 equal portions from the salmon mixture and shape them into patties, measuring approximately 3-4 inches in diameter.
4. Cover both sides of the salmon cakes in all-purpose flour by dredging them in a shallow dish.

5. In a large skillet, heat olive oil over medium heat. Carefully add the floured salmon cakes in batches, cooking for 2-3 minutes per side or until golden brown.
6. Move the seared salmon cakes to the baking sheet. Bake until cooked through and crispy, about 10-12 minutes in the preheated oven.
7. As the salmon cakes bake, make the dill lemon sauce. Whisk together Greek yogurt, lemon juice, chopped dill, and minced garlic in a small bowl. Season with salt and pepper to taste.
8. Serve the baked salmon cakes warm, drizzled with the Dill Lemon Sauce. Enjoy!

Nutritional breakdown per serving:

Calories: 380 kcal, Protein: 29 grams, Carbohydrates: 26 grams, Fat: 18 grams, Saturated Fat: 3 grams, Cholesterol: 90 milligrams, Sodium: 540 milligrams, Fiber: 2 grams, and Sugar: 2 grams.

SAUTÉED SHRIMP WITH GARLIC, LEMON, AND PARSLEY

Total Time: 20 minutes
Prep Time: 10 minutes
Servings: 4

Ingredients:

- 1 lb large shrimp, peeled and deveined
- 3 tablespoons olive oil
- 4 garlic cloves, minced
- 1/4 cup freshly squeezed lemon juice
- 2 tablespoons chopped fresh parsley
- 1 teaspoon lemon zest
- Salt and black pepper to taste
- Lemon wedges, for serving

Instructions:

1. Season the dried shrimp with a sprinkle of salt and pepper.
2. A large frying pan, heated over medium-high heat, should contain olive oil.
3. Stir minced garlic into the hot oil for 1 minute until fragrant.
4. Sauté the seasoned shrimp in the skillet for 2-3 minutes per side, or until cooked through and opaque.
5. After cooking the shrimp, add freshly squeezed lemon juice, chopped parsley, and lemon zest to the skillet. Add salt and black pepper to taste.
6. Serve the Sautéed Shrimp with Garlic, Lemon, and Parsley immediately, garnished with lemon wedges. Enjoy with crusty bread, over pasta, or alongside a fresh salad.

Nutritional breakdown per serving:

Calories: 195 kcal, Protein: 21 grams, Carbohydrates: 4 grams, Fat: 11 grams, Saturated Fat: 1.5 grams, Cholesterol: 215 milligrams, Sodium: 370 milligrams, Fiber: 0 grams, and Sugar: 1 grams.

POACHED TUNA SALAD WITH OLIVES AND ROASTED PEPPERS

Total Time: 30 minutes
Prep Time: 20 minutes
Servings: 4

Ingredients:

- 1 lb fresh tuna steak
- 2 cups water
- 2 tablespoons white wine vinegar
- 1 bay leaf
- 2 sprigs fresh thyme
- 1/2 cup mixed olives, pitted and halved
- 1/2 cup roasted red peppers, sliced
- 2 tablespoons olive oil
- 1 tablespoon Dijon mustard
- 2 tablespoons lemon juice
- 1/4 cup chopped fresh parsley
- Salt and black pepper to taste
- Mixed greens or lettuce, for serving

Instructions:

1. Combine water, white wine vinegar, bay leaf, and thyme sprigs in a medium saucepan and simmer over medium heat.
2. Carefully add the tuna steak to the simmering liquid, making sure it is completely submerged. Poach the tuna for 8-10 minutes, or until it is opaque and cooked through.
3. Once the tuna is poached, take it out of the liquid and let it cool down a bit. Once cool enough to handle, flake the tuna into large chunks.
4. Toss flaked tuna, olives, roasted red peppers, olive oil, Dijon mustard, lemon juice, and chopped parsley in a large bowl until combined.
5. Add salt and pepper to taste.
6. Serve poached tuna salad with olives and roasted peppers over a bed of mixed greens or lettuce.

Nutritional breakdown per serving:

Calories: 260 kcal, Protein: 26 grams, Carbohydrates: 8 grams, Fat: 14 grams, Saturated Fat: 2 grams, Cholesterol: 45 milligrams, Sodium: 590 milligrams, Fiber: 2 grams, and Sugar: 2 grams.

BAKED COD WITH TOMATO, CAPER, AND OLIVE RELISH

Total Time: 40 minutes
Prep Time: 20 minutes
Servings: 4

Ingredients:

Tomato, Caper, and Olive Relish:

- 1 cup diced tomatoes (about 2 medium tomatoes)
- 1/4 cup chopped kalamata olives, pitted
- 2 tablespoons capers, rinsed and chopped
- 2 tablespoons chopped fresh parsley
- 1 tablespoon olive oil
- 1 tablespoon red wine vinegar
- 1 garlic clove, minced
- Salt and black pepper to taste

Baked Cod:

- 4 (6 oz) cod fillets
- 2 tablespoons olive oil
- Salt and black pepper to taste

Instructions:

Tomato, Caper, and Olive Relish:

1. In a medium bowl, toss together diced tomatoes, chopped olives, capers, chopped parsley, olive oil, red wine vinegar, and minced garlic.
2. Before preparing the cod, season the relish with salt and pepper and set it aside, covered.

Baked Cod:

3. Begin by adjusting the oven temperature to 400°F (200°C).
4. Cod fillets should be patted dry with paper towels and seasoned with salt and pepper.

5. A large, oven-safe skillet or baking dish, heated over medium-high heat, should contain 2 tablespoons of olive oil.

6. Add the seasoned cod fillets to the hot oil and sear for 2-3 minutes per side, or until the fish is lightly browned.

7. Bake the cod until it is cooked through and no longer translucent.

8. Garnish each baked cod fillet with a generous amount of the tomato, caper, and olive relish.

9. Serve the Baked Cod with Tomato, Caper, and Olive Relish immediately, garnished with additional chopped parsley if desired.

Nutritional breakdown per serving:

Calories: 260 kcal, Protein: 29 grams, Carbohydrates: 8 grams, Fat: 12 grams, Saturated Fat: 2 grams, Cholesterol: 65 milligrams, Sodium: 590 milligrams, Fiber: 2 grams, and Sugar: 3 grams.

GRILLED SWORDFISH STEAKS WITH CUCUMBER SALAD

Total Time: 30 minutes
Prep Time: 20 minutes
Servings: 4

Ingredients:

Cucumber Salad:

- 2 cucumbers, peeled, seeded, and sliced
- 1/2 red onion, thinly sliced
- 2 tablespoons red wine vinegar
- 1 tablespoon olive oil
- 1 tablespoon chopped fresh dill
- Salt and black pepper to taste

Grilled Swordfish:

- 4 (6 oz) swordfish steaks
- 2 tablespoons olive oil
- 2 teaspoons lemon zest
- 1 teaspoon dried oregano
- Salt and black pepper to taste

Instructions:

Cucumber Salad:

1. A medium bowl can be used to mix together sliced cucumbers, sliced red onion, red wine vinegar, olive oil, and chopped fresh dill.
2. Season the cucumber salad with salt and black pepper to taste. Cover and refrigerate until ready to serve.

Grilled Swordfish:

3. Grill or grill pan, preheated to medium-high.

4. Swordfish steaks should be patted dry with paper towels and placed in a shallow baking dish.

5. Drizzle the swordfish steaks with the 2 tablespoons of olive oil and sprinkle with the lemon zest, dried oregano, salt, and black pepper. Gently rub the seasonings into the fish.

6. Grill the swordfish steaks until they are cooked through and no longer translucent.

7. Remove the grilled swordfish steaks from the grill and let them rest for a few minutes.

8. To serve, place the grilled swordfish steaks on plates and top with the chilled Cucumber Salad.

Nutritional breakdown per serving:

Calories: 270 kcal, Protein: 32 grams, Carbohydrates: 8 grams, Fat: 12 grams, Saturated Fat: 2 grams, Cholesterol: 55 milligrams, Sodium: 220 milligrams, Fiber: 2 grams, and Sugar: 3 grams.

MEDITERRANEAN BAKED TILAPIA WITH ARTICHOKES AND LEMON

Total Time: 35 minutes
Prep Time: 15 minutes
Servings: 4

Ingredients:

- 4 (6 oz) tilapia fillets
- 14 oz can artichoke hearts, quartered
- 1 lemon, zested and juiced
- 2 tablespoons olive oil
- 3 cloves garlic, minced
- 1/4 cup chopped fresh parsley
- 1/4 cup chopped kalamata olives, pitted
- 1 teaspoon dried oregano
- Salt and black pepper to taste

Instructions:

1. Begin by adjusting the oven temperature to 400°F (200°C).
2. Place the tilapia fillets in a single layer on a large baking dish or a rimmed baking sheet.
3. In a medium bowl, combine the quartered artichoke hearts, lemon zest, lemon juice, olive oil, minced garlic, chopped parsley, chopped kalamata olives, and dried oregano. Stir to mix well.
4. Spoon the artichoke mixture evenly over the top of the tilapia fillets, making sure to distribute the ingredients evenly.
5. Sprinkle salt and black pepper on the dish to suit your taste.
6. Gently bake the Mediterranean Baked Tilapia with Artichokes and Lemon until the fish is cooked through and has an opaque appearance. This should take about 18-22 minutes.
7. Remove the dish from the oven and let it cool for a few minutes.
8. Serve the Mediterranean Baked Tilapia with Artichokes and Lemon immediately, garnished with additional chopped parsley if desired.

Nutritional breakdown per serving:

Calories: 260 kcal, Protein: 28 grams, Carbohydrates: 10 grams, Fat: 11 grams, Saturated Fat: 2 grams, Cholesterol: 65 milligrams, Sodium: 580 milligrams, Fiber: 4 grams, and Sugar: 2 grams.

SEARED AHI TUNA WITH AVOCADO AND GRAPEFRUIT SALAD

Total Time: 30 minutes
Prep Time: 20 minutes
Servings: 4

Ingredients:

Salad:

- 2 grapefruit, peeled and segmented
- 1 avocado, diced
- 1/2 red onion, thinly sliced
- 2 tablespoons olive oil
- 1 tablespoon white wine vinegar
- 1 teaspoon honey
- Salt and black pepper to taste

Seared Ahi Tuna:

- 4 (6 oz) ahi tuna steaks
- 2 tablespoons olive oil
- 1 tablespoon sesame seeds
- 1 teaspoon ground cumin
- 1/2 teaspoon chili powder
- Salt and black pepper to taste

Instructions:

Salad:

1. Toss the grapefruit segments, diced avocado, and thinly sliced red onion in a medium bowl.

2. Create a vinaigrette by whisking together 2 tablespoons olive oil, white wine vinegar, and honey.

3. Spoon the dressing onto the salad and softly combine to blend. Add salt and pepper to taste.

4. Seal the salad and place it in the refrigerator until you're ready to serve.

Seared Ahi Tuna:

5. Dab the ahi tuna steaks with paper towels to remove moisture, then season all sides with sesame seeds, ground cumin, chili powder, salt, and black pepper.

6. Using a large skillet or grill pan, heat 2 tablespoons of olive oil over high heat.

7. When the oil is hot, add the seasoned ahi tuna steaks and sear them for 2-3 minutes per side, or until the outside is nicely browned and the center is still rare to medium-rare.

8. Remove the seared ahi tuna steaks from the heat and let them rest for a few minutes.

9. To serve, place the seared ahi tuna steaks on plates and top with the chilled Avocado and Grapefruit Salad.

Nutritional breakdown per serving:

Calories: 350 kcal, Protein: 30 grams, Carbohydrates: 18 grams, Fat: 19 grams, Saturated Fat: 3 grams, Cholesterol: 45 milligrams, Sodium: 260 milligrams, Fiber: 5 grams, and Sugar: 9 grams.

ROASTED SALMON WITH MEDITERRANEAN QUINOA SALAD

Total Time: 45 minutes
Prep Time: 30 minutes
Servings: 4

Ingredients:

Salmon:

- 4 (6 oz) salmon fillets
- 2 tablespoons olive oil
- 1 teaspoon dried oregano
- 1/2 teaspoon garlic powder
- Salt and black pepper to taste

Quinoa Salad:

- 1 cup uncooked quinoa, rinsed
- 1 cup cherry tomatoes, halved
- 1 cucumber, diced
- 1/2 cup crumbled feta cheese
- 2 tablespoons pitted and halved kalamata olives
- 2 tablespoons chopped fresh parsley
- 2 tablespoons lemon juice
- 1 tablespoon olive oil
- 1 teaspoon dried oregano
- Salt and black pepper to taste

Instructions:

Salmon:

1. Begin by adjusting the oven temperature to 400°F (200°C).

2. Carefully place the salmon fillets on a baking sheet prepared with parchment paper.

3. Season the salmon with oregano, garlic powder, salt, and pepper, then drizzle with olive oil.

4. Bake the salmon in the preheated oven until it flakes easily with a fork, which should take about 12-15 minutes.

Quinoa Salad:

5. Begin cooking by bringing 2 cups of water to a boil in a medium saucepan. Add the rinsed quinoa, reduce the heat to low, cover, and simmer until the quinoa is tender and the water has been absorbed. This should take about 15-20 minutes.

6. Move the cooked quinoa to a large bowl and allow it to cool for a few minutes.

7. Add the halved cherry tomatoes, diced cucumber, crumbled feta cheese, halved kalamata olives, and chopped fresh parsley to the bowl with the quinoa.

8. Create a flavorful dressing by combining lemon juice, olive oil, oregano, salt, and pepper in a small bowl and whisking until well blended.

9. Toss the quinoa salad with the prepared dressing.

To Serve:

10. Divide the roasted salmon fillets among 4 plates.

11. Spoon the Mediterranean Quinoa Salad alongside the salmon.

12. Serve immediately, garnished with additional fresh parsley if desired.

Nutritional breakdown per serving:

Calories: 440 kcal, Protein: 35 grams, Carbohydrates: 27 grams, Fat: 22 grams, Saturated Fat: 5 grams, Cholesterol: 75 milligrams, Sodium: 590 milligrams, Fiber: 5 grams, and Sugar: 3 grams.

GRILLED OCTOPUS WITH LEMON AND OREGANO

Total Time: 1 hour 15 minutes
Prep Time: 45 minutes
Servings: 4

Ingredients:

- 1 lb octopus, cleaned and tentacles separated
- 1/4 cup olive oil, with additional oil for grilling as needed
- 2 tablespoons freshly squeezed lemon juice
- 2 tablespoons chopped fresh oregano
- 1 teaspoon grated lemon zest
- 1/2 teaspoon red pepper flakes
- Salt and black pepper to taste

Instructions:

1. In a large pot of boiling salted water, add the octopus tentacles. Cook until the octopus is tender, which should take about 45-60 minutes. Drain the octopus and let it cool slightly before proceeding.
2. In a large bowl, whisk together the 1/4 cup of olive oil, lemon juice, oregano, lemon zest, and red pepper flakes. Add salt and pepper to taste.
3. Add the cooked octopus tentacles to the bowl with the lemon-oregano dressing and toss to coat evenly. Let the dish chill in the refrigerator, covered, for at least 30 minutes, or up to 4 hours, to develop the flavors.
4. Grill or grill pan, preheated to medium-high. Grease the grill grates or pan with a thin layer of olive oil.
5. Prepare your grill or grill pan by preheating it to medium-high and lightly brushing the grates or pan with olive oil.
6. Remove the grilled octopus from the heat and transfer to a serving plate. Drizzle any remaining lemon-oregano dressing from the bowl over the top.
7. Serve the Grilled Octopus with Lemon and Oregano immediately, while it's hot and fresh off the grill.

Nutritional breakdown per serving:

Calories: 170 kcal, Protein: 19 grams, Carbohydrates: 3 grams, Fat: 9 grams, Saturated Fat: 1 grams, Cholesterol: 125 milligrams, Sodium: 390 milligrams, Fiber: 0 grams, and Sugar: 0 grams.

BAKED HADDOCK WITH TOMATO AND BASIL TOPPING

Total Time: 30 minutes
Prep Time: 15 minutes
Servings: 4

Ingredients:

- 4 (6 oz) haddock fillets
- 2 tablespoons olive oil
- 2 cloves garlic, minced
- 1 cup cherry tomatoes, halved
- 1/4 cup fresh basil leaves, chopped
- 2 tablespoons Parmesan cheese, grated
- Salt and black pepper to taste

Instructions:

1. Begin by adjusting the oven temperature to 400°F (200°C).
2. Position the haddock fillets in a baking dish or on a parchment-lined baking sheet.
3. Make a garlic-olive oil glaze by combining olive oil and minced garlic in a small bowl and whisking to combine. Drizzle the glaze evenly over the haddock fillets.
4. In another bowl, mix together the halved cherry tomatoes, chopped fresh basil, and grated Parmesan cheese. Season with salt and black pepper.
5. Spoon the tomato and basil topping over the haddock fillets, gently spreading it to cover the top of each fillet.
6. Bake the haddock until it reaches an internal temperature of 145°F (63°C) and the topping is lightly golden, which should take about 12-15 minutes.
7. Remove the baked haddock from the oven and let it rest for a few minutes before serving.

Nutritional breakdown per serving:

Calories: 220 kcal, Protein: 26 grams, Carbohydrates: 6 grams, Fat: 10 grams, Saturated Fat: 2 grams, Cholesterol: 65 milligrams, Sodium: 330 milligrams, Fiber: 1 grams, and Sugar: 2 grams.

SAUTÉED SHRIMP SCAMPI WITH ZUCCHINI NOODLES

Total Time: 30 minutes
Prep Time: 20 minutes
Servings: 4

Ingredients:

- 1 lb large shrimp, peeled and deveined
- 3 tablespoons olive oil, divided
- 4 cloves garlic, minced
- 1/4 cup dry white wine
- 2 tablespoons freshly squeezed lemon juice
- 2 tablespoons unsalted butter
- 2 tablespoons chopped fresh parsley
- Salt and black pepper to taste
- 3 medium zucchini, spiralized or julienned into noodles
- 1/4 cup grated Parmesan cheese (optional)

Instructions:

1. In a large skillet, use medium-high heat to warm 2 tablespoons of olive oil.
2. Add the shrimp to the skillet and sauté for 2-3 minutes per side, or until the shrimp are opaque and slightly curled. Place the cooked shrimp on a plate and let it cool.
3. Using the same skillet, warm 1 tablespoon of olive oil over medium heat. Next, add the minced garlic and sauté it for 1 minute, or until fragrant.
4. Simmer white wine and lemon juice in the skillet for 2-3 minutes, scraping up any browned bits on the bottom.
5. Turn down the heat to low and stir in the unsalted butter until it melts and is fully combined.
6. Toss the cooked shrimp and chopped fresh parsley together in the skillet, then season with salt and pepper.
7. In a separate skillet or saucepan, heat the spiralized or julienned zucchini noodles over medium-high heat for 2-3 minutes, or until they are tender but still have a slight bite.
8. Divide the zucchini noodles among serving plates and top with the sautéed shrimp scampi.
9. (Optional) Sprinkle the Parmesan cheese over the top of the dish before serving.

Nutritional breakdown per serving:

Calories: 240 kcal, Protein: 21 grams, Carbohydrates: 9 grams, Fat: 14 grams, Saturated Fat: 4 grams, Cholesterol: 185 milligrams, Sodium: 480 milligrams, Fiber: 2 grams, and Sugar: 5 grams.

POACHED HALIBUT WITH FENNEL AND ORANGE SALSA

Total Time: 40 minutes
Prep Time: 25 minutes
Servings: 4

Ingredients:

Fennel and Orange Salsa:

- 1 medium fennel bulb, thinly sliced
- 1 orange, peeled and segmented
- 1/4 cup fresh cilantro, chopped
- 2 tablespoons olive oil
- 1 tablespoon white wine vinegar
- Salt and black pepper to taste

Poached Halibut:

- 4 (6 oz) halibut fillets
- 4 cups low-sodium chicken or vegetable broth
- 2 bay leaves
- 1 teaspoon whole black peppercorns
- 1 tablespoon fresh lemon juice

Instructions:

Fennel and Orange Salsa:

1. In a medium bowl, whisk together thinly sliced fennel, orange segments, chopped cilantro, olive oil, and white wine vinegar. Season to taste with salt and pepper. Gently toss to combine.

Poached Halibut:

2. In a large skillet or saucepan, bring the broth, bay leaves, and peppercorns to a gentle simmer over medium heat.

3. Carefully add the halibut fillets to the simmering broth, making sure they are submerged. Poach the halibut until it reaches an internal temperature of 145°F (63°C), which should take about 10-12 minutes.

4. Using a slotted spoon, gently transfer the poached halibut fillets to a serving plate.

5. Drizzle the poached halibut with the fresh lemon juice.

6. Top the halibut with the prepared fennel and orange salsa, making sure to evenly distribute the salsa over the fish.

Nutritional breakdown per serving:

Calories: 270 kcal, Protein: 32 grams, Carbohydrates: 12 grams, Fat: 10 grams, Saturated Fat: 2 grams, Cholesterol: 55 milligrams, Sodium: 500 milligrams, Fiber: 3 grams, and Sugar: 6 grams.

CHAPTER 6
DESSERTS AND BAKED TREATS

MEDITERRANEAN LEMON OLIVE OIL CAKE

Total Cooking Time: 1 hour
Prep Time: 20 minutes
Servings: 12 (1 slice per serving)

Ingredients:

Cake:

- 1 1/2 cups all-purpose flour
- 1 teaspoon baking powder
- 1/4 teaspoon salt
- 3 large eggs
- 1 cup granulated sugar
- 3/4 cup extra-virgin olive oil
- 1/4 cup fresh lemon juice
- 2 tablespoons lemon zest (from the same 2 lemons)
- 1 teaspoon vanilla extract

Lemon Glaze:

- 1 cup confectioners' sugar
- 2-3 tablespoons fresh lemon juice
- 1 tablespoon lemon zest

Directions:

1. Begin by setting your oven temperature to 350°F (175°C). Lightly coat the interior of a 9-inch round baking pan with a thin layer of grease or cooking spray. Then, dust the greased surface with a light coating of flour.
2. Take a medium-sized mixing bowl and, using a whisk, blend together the all-purpose flour, baking powder, and salt until the dry ingredients are thoroughly combined.
3. Beat the eggs and granulated sugar vigorously with an electric mixer in a large bowl until the mixture is light and fluffy. This process will take approximately 3-5 minutes.
4. Turn the mixer speed to low and gradually pour in the olive oil, lemon juice, lemon zest, and vanilla extract. Mix until the ingredients are thoroughly combined.
5. Gently fold the dry ingredients from step 2 into the wet ingredients until just combined.
6. Transfer the batter to the prepared 9-inch round pan, spreading it evenly.

7. Once the oven has preheated, carefully place the prepared baking pan inside. Once the oven has preheated to the appropriate temperature, carefully transfer the pan containing the prepared cake batter into the oven. Let the cake bake for 35 to 40 minutes.
8. Take the baked cake out of the oven and place the pan on a heat-safe surface. After the cake has finished baking, leave it in the pan and allow it to rest on the countertop for approximately 10 minutes.
9. Prepare the lemon glaze by gathering a small mixing bowl. Gather a small mixing bowl, then add the confectioners' sugar, 2 tablespoons of freshly squeezed lemon juice, and lemon zest to the bowl. Mix these ingredients together until they form a smooth, uniform glaze.
10. Take the lemon glaze you previously prepared and slowly pour it over the top of the cooled cake. Let the glaze naturally flow and drip down the sides of the cake, creating an attractive and glossy finish.
11. Serve the Mediterranean Lemon Olive Oil Cake at room temperature.

Nutritional breakdown per serving:

Calories: 280 kcal, Protein: 3 grams, Carbohydrates: 35 grams, Fat: 14 grams, Saturated Fat: 2 grams, Cholesterol: 45, Sodium: 100 milligrams, Fiber: 1 grams, and Sugar: 5 grams.

BAKLAVA BITES

Total Cooking Time: 1 hour 15 minutes
Prep Time: 30 minutes
Servings: 24 (1 bite per serving)

Ingredients:

Filling:

- 1 cup chopped walnuts
- 1/2 cup chopped pistachios
- 1/4 cup brown sugar
- 1 teaspoon ground cinnamon
- 1/2 teaspoon ground cloves

Dough:

- 1 sheet frozen phyllo dough, thawed
- 1/2 cup unsalted butter, melted

Syrup:

- 1/2 cup honey
- 2 tablespoons lemon juice
- 1 tablespoon water

Directions:

1. Get started by setting your oven temperature to 350°F (175°C). Grease a 24-cup mini muffin tin.
2. In a food processor, pulse the walnuts, pistachios, brown sugar, cinnamon, and cloves until finely chopped. Scoop the prepared filling mixture into a separate bowl and set it aside for later use.
3. Unroll the thawed phyllo dough and cut it into 24 squares, approximately 3-inch by 3-inch each.
4. Brush each muffin cup with melted butter. Take one sheet of phyllo dough and place it into each cup of a muffin tin. Gently press the phyllo dough down into the bottom of the cup and up along the sides, molding it to create a small, cup-shaped shell.
5. Spoon about 1 tablespoon of the nut filling into each phyllo cup.

6. Gather a small saucepan and add the honey, lemon juice, and water. Heat the saucepan over medium heat, simmering the honey, lemon juice, and water mixture while stirring occasionally, until the honey dissolves and the syrup slightly thickens, about 5 minutes.
7. Drizzle about 1 teaspoon of the warm honey syrup over the filling in each phyllo cup.
8. Once the oven has preheated to the proper temperature, carefully place the Baklava Bites inside and allow them to bake for 20 to 25 minutes.
9. Once the baking time is up, carefully remove the muffin tin containing the Baklava Bites from the oven. Let the pastries cool within the tin for 10 minutes before taking them out.
10. After the Baklava Bites have cooled in the muffin tin for 10 minutes, gently remove them from the tin and transfer the individual pastries to a serving platter.
11. Serve the Baklava Bites warm or at room temperature.

Nutritional breakdown per serving:

Calories: 100 kcal, Protein: 1 grams, Carbohydrates: 12 grams, Fat: 6 grams, Saturated Fat: 2 grams, Cholesterol: 5 milligrams, Sodium: 5 milligrams, Fiber: 1 grams, and Sugar: 5 grams.

PISTACHIO AND HONEY YOGURT PARFAITS

Total Cooking Time: 15 minutes
Prep Time: 10 minutes
Servings: 4 (1 parfait per serving)

Ingredients:

- 2 cups plain Greek yogurt
- 1/4 cup honey, plus extra for drizzling
- 1 cup shelled pistachios, roughly chopped
- 1 cup granola (your favorite brand)

Directions:

1. Take a medium-sized bowl and add the Greek yogurt and 1/4 cup of honey. Combine the ingredients in the bowl and mix them together thoroughly until they are well blended and the mixture has a smooth, uniform consistency.
2. In a separate bowl, combine the chopped pistachios and granola.
3. To assemble the parfaits, layer the yogurt mixture and the pistachio-granola mixture in 4 glasses or jars, starting and ending with the yogurt mixture.
4. Drizzle a small amount of additional honey over the top of each parfait.
5. Before serving the parfaits, place them in the refrigerator and let them chill for a minimum of 30 minutes. This resting period enables the flavors within the parfaits to fully blend and marry together.

Nutritional breakdown per serving:

Calories: 320 kcal, Protein: 15 grams, Carbohydrates: 35 grams, Fat: 14 grams, Saturated Fat: 2 grams, Cholesterol: 10 milligrams, Sodium: 80 milligrams, Fiber: 3 grams, and Sugar: 5 grams.

BAKED MEDITERRANEAN FIG AND ALMOND STUFFED APPLES

Total Cooking Time: 45 minutes
Prep Time: 15 minutes
Servings: 4 (1 stuffed apple per serving)

Ingredients:

- 4 medium-sized Honeycrisp or Gala apples
- 1/2 cup chopped dried figs
- 1/4 cup chopped roasted almonds
- 2 tablespoons honey
- 1 teaspoon ground cinnamon
- 1/4 teaspoon ground nutmeg
- 2 tablespoons unsalted butter, melted

Directions:

1. Get started by setting your oven temperature to 375°F (190°C).
2. Slice the tops off the apples and use a melon baller or small spoon to carefully scoop out the cores, leaving about a 1/2-inch wall on the bottom and sides of each apple.
3. In a small bowl, mix together the chopped dried figs, chopped almonds, honey, cinnamon, and nutmeg until well combined.
4. Spoon the fig-almond mixture evenly into the hollowed-out apples.
5. Place the prepared stuffed apples into a baking dish. Once they are arranged in the dish, drizzle the melted butter over the top of the apples, coating them evenly.
6. Preheat the oven, then transfer the stuffed apples to a baking dish and place them in the hot oven. Allow the apples to bake for 30 to 35 minutes, or until they become tender and the filling is thoroughly heated.
7. Once the Baked Mediterranean Fig and Almond Stuffed Apples have finished cooking, serve them warm. For an added touch, you can drizzle a bit of extra honey over the top or provide a dollop of Greek yogurt alongside the apples, if desired.

Nutritional breakdown per serving:

Calories: 220 kcal, Protein: 2 grams, Carbohydrates: 35 grams, Fat: 8 grams, Saturated Fat: 3 grams, Cholesterol: 10 milligrams, Sodium: 5 milligrams, Fiber: 5 grams, and Sugar: 5 grams.

MEDITERRANEAN ORANGE AND ALMOND BISCOTTI

Total Cooking Time: 1 hour
Prep Time: 20 minutes
Servings: 24 (1 biscotti per serving)

Ingredients:

- 2 cups all-purpose flour
- 1 teaspoon baking powder
- 1/4 teaspoon salt
- 3/4 cup granulated sugar
- 2 large eggs
- 1 tablespoon grated orange zest
- 1 teaspoon vanilla extract
- 1 cup toasted almonds, chopped

Directions:

1. Get started by setting your oven temperature to 325°F (165°C). Line a baking sheet with parchment paper.
2. Grab a medium-sized bowl and add the flour, baking powder, and salt. Using a whisk, mix these dry ingredients together until they are well incorporated. Once combined, set the bowl aside for later use.
3. In a large bowl, mix the sugar and eggs together. Use a hand or stand mixer to beat the ingredients for about 2-3 minutes, until the mixture becomes light and airy in texture.
4. Introduce the orange zest and vanilla extract to the bowl, then stir the mixture until the added ingredients are thoroughly combined.
5. In the bowl with the wet ingredients, slowly add the dry ingredients, mixing them together only until they are just combined. Once that's done, gently fold in the chopped and toasted almonds.
6. Take the dough and divide it evenly into two halves. Shape each half into a log that is approximately 1-inch tall and 12 inches long. Place the shaped dough logs onto the prepared baking sheet, ensuring they are spaced about 4 inches apart from one another.

7. Once the dough logs have been arranged on the prepared baking sheet, place the sheet in the preheated oven. Bake the logs for 25 minutes, or until they develop a light golden brown color.
8. Retrieve the baking sheet from the oven after the dough logs have finished baking. Once the baking is complete, leave the dough logs on the baking sheet and let them cool for 10 minutes before handling or moving them.
9. Grab a serrated knife and use it to slice the cooled dough logs diagonally into biscotti pieces that are approximately 1/2-inch thick.
10. Once the dough logs have been sliced into 1/2-inch thick biscotti pieces using the serrated knife, arrange the sliced biscotti on the baking sheet with the cut-sides facing down.
11. Put the sliced biscotti back on the baking sheet, cut-side down. Then, return the sheet to the oven and continue baking the biscotti for 12-15 more minutes, flipping them over halfway through the time, until they become crisp and a golden brown color.
12. Transfer the baked biscotti to a wire rack to cool completely before serving.

Nutritional breakdown per serving:

Calories: 110 kcal, Protein: 3 grams, Carbohydrates: 16 grams, Fat: 4 grams, Saturated Fat: 0.5 grams, Cholesterol: 15 milligrams, Sodium: 45 milligrams, Fiber: 1 grams, and Sugar: 5 grams.

GRILLED MEDITERRANEAN FRUIT SKEWERS WITH HONEY-LEMON DRIZZLE

Total Cooking Time: 25 minutes
Prep Time: 15 minutes
Servings: 6 (2 skewers per serving)

Ingredients:

- 1 pint fresh strawberries, washed and halved
- 1 pint fresh blackberries
- 1 medium mango, peeled and cubed
- 1 cup cubed fresh pineapple
- 1 cup seedless grapes
- 12 wooden skewers, pre-soaked for 30 minutes
- 1/4 cup honey
- 2 tablespoons fresh lemon juice

Directions:

1. Prepare the grill or grill pan by preheating it to medium-high heat.
2. Thread the strawberries, blackberries, mango cubes, pineapple, and grapes onto the soaked wooden skewers, alternating the fruits.
3. In a small bowl, whisk together the honey and lemon juice until well combined.
4. Once the grill or grill pan is preheated, place the fruit skewers on it and cook for 2-3 minutes per side, or until the fruit becomes slightly charred and softened.
5. Transfer the grilled fruit skewers to a serving platter.
6. Drizzle the honey-lemon mixture over the top of the warm fruit skewers.
7. Serve the Grilled Mediterranean Fruit Skewers warm, with the honey-lemon drizzle.

Nutritional breakdown per serving:

Calories: 170 kcal, Protein: 2 grams, Carbohydrates: 44 grams, Fat: 0 grams, Saturated Fat: 0 grams, Cholesterol: 0 milligrams, Sodium: 5 milligrams, Fiber: 5 grams, and Sugar: 5 grams.

MEDITERRANEAN OLIVE OIL AND ROSEMARY SHORTBREAD COOKIES

Total Cooking Time: 35 minutes
Prep Time: 20 minutes
Servings: 18 (1 cookie per serving)

Ingredients:

- 1 3/4 cups all-purpose flour
- 1/4 cup granulated sugar
- 1/2 teaspoon salt
- 2 tablespoons fresh rosemary, finely chopped
- 1/2 cup extra-virgin olive oil
- 2 tablespoons cold water

Directions:

1. Get started by setting your oven temperature to 350°F (175°C). Line a baking sheet with parchment paper.
2. Take a large bowl and use a whisk to combine the flour, sugar, salt, and chopped rosemary.
3. Gather the dry ingredients and place them in a mixing bowl. Add the olive oil and cold water, then use a fork or your fingers to mix everything together until a dough forms.
4. Move the dough to a lightly floured work surface and gently knead it a few times to fully combine the ingredients.
5. On the floured surface, roll the dough out until it reaches approximately 1/4-inch thickness.
6. To create the shortbread cookies, use a 2-inch round cookie cutter. Re-roll the dough as needed to use it all up.
7. Position the cut-out cookie shapes on the prepared baking sheet, leaving approximately 1 inch of space between each one.
8. After preheating the oven, put the baking sheet in and allow the cookies to bake for 12-15 minutes, until their edges have taken on a light golden color.
9. Once the baking time is up, take the cookies out of the oven and let them cool on the baking sheet for about 5 minutes. After letting the cookies rest on the baking sheet for a few minutes, gently transfer them to a wire rack to cool completely.

Nutritional breakdown per serving:

Calories: 110 kcal, Protein: 1 grams, Carbohydrates: 13 grams, Fat: 6 grams, Saturated Fat: 1 grams, Cholesterol: 0 milligrams, Sodium: 75 milligrams, Fiber: 0 grams, and Sugar: 5 grams.

CREAMY MEDITERRANEAN LEMON CHEESECAKE BARS

Total Cooking Time: 1 hour 30 minutes
Prep Time: 30 minutes
Servings: 16 (1 bar per serving)

Ingredients:

Crust:

- 1 1/2 cups graham cracker crumbs
- 5 tablespoons unsalted butter, melted

Filling:

- 16 ounces cream cheese, softened
- 3/4 cup granulated sugar
- 2 tablespoons all-purpose flour
- 1/4 cup fresh lemon juice
- 2 teaspoons grated lemon zest
- 2 large eggs
- 1/2 cup plain Greek yogurt

Topping:

- 1/2 cup fresh raspberries
- 2 tablespoons honey

Directions:

1. Get started by setting your oven temperature to 325°F (160°C). To make cleanup easier, line your 8-inch square baking pan with parchment paper, allowing a portion to extend beyond the edges.
2. Press a mixture of crushed graham crackers and melted butter firmly into the prepared baking pan.
3. Bake the crust until golden brown, about 8 minutes. Let it cool completely.
4. In a large bowl, use an electric mixer to whip the cream cheese until it reaches a smooth, creamy consistency. Then, slowly incorporate the sugar and flour, continuing to mix everything together until well combined.

5. Take a medium-sized bowl and add the ricotta cheese, 2 tablespoons of honey, vanilla extract, and cinnamon. Mix all of these ingredients together thoroughly until they are fully combined.
6. Carefully pour the cheesecake filling over the cooled crust, then use a spatula to spread it evenly.
7. Bake for 40-45 minutes, or until the center is almost set. The center should still be slightly jiggly.
8. Turn off the oven and leave the cheesecake bars in the oven for 1 hour.
9. After the cheesecake bars have finished baking, take them out of the oven and let them cool down completely on a wire rack.
10. Once cooled, refrigerate the bars for at least 2 hours (or up to 3 days).
11. Just before serving, top the chilled cheesecake bars with fresh raspberries and drizzle with honey.

Nutritional breakdown per serving:

Calories: 200 kcal, Protein: 4 grams, Carbohydrates: 20 grams, Fat: ë1 grams, Saturated Fat: 7 grams, Cholesterol: 55 milligrams, Sodium: 130 milligrams, Fiber: 1 grams, and Sugar: 5 grams.

BAKED MEDITERRANEAN RICOTTA AND HONEY STUFFED FIGS

Total Cooking Time: 30 minutes
Prep Time: 15 minutes
Servings: 12 (1 stuffed fig per serving)

Ingredients:

- 12 fresh figs, halved lengthwise
- 1 cup whole milk ricotta cheese
- 2 tablespoons honey, plus more for drizzling
- 1 teaspoon vanilla extract
- 1/4 teaspoon ground cinnamon
- 2 tablespoons chopped pistachios
- 2 tablespoons crumbled feta cheese

Directions:

1. Get started by setting your oven temperature to 375°F (190°C). Line a baking sheet with parchment paper.
2. Take a medium-sized bowl and add the ricotta cheese, 2 tablespoons of honey, vanilla extract, and cinnamon. Mix all of these ingredients together thoroughly until they are fully combined.
3. Carefully spoon or pipe the ricotta mixture into the center of each fig half, dividing it evenly among the 24 fig halves.
4. Arrange the stuffed fig halves on the prepared baking sheet.
5. Bake for 12-15 minutes, or until the figs are softened and the ricotta filling is lightly browned.
6. Remove the baked stuffed figs from the oven and let them cool for 5 minutes.
7. Drizzle the warm stuffed figs with additional honey and sprinkle with the chopped pistachios and crumbled feta cheese.
8. Serve the Baked Mediterranean Ricotta and Honey Stuffed Figs warm.

Nutritional breakdown per serving:

Calories: 80 kcal, Protein: 3 grams, Carbohydrates: 11 grams, Fat: 3 grams, Saturated Fat: 2 grams, Cholesterol: 10 milligrams, Sodium: 50 milligrams, Fiber: 2 grams, and Sugar: 5 grams.

MEDITERRANEAN ALMOND AND ORANGE SEMOLINA CAKE

Total Cooking Time: 1 hour 15 minutes
Prep Time: 30 minutes
Servings: 12 (1 slice per serving)

Ingredients:

Cake:

- 1 cup semolina flour
- 1 cup almond flour
- 1 teaspoon baking powder
- 1/4 teaspoon salt
- 3 large eggs
- 3/4 cup granulated sugar
- 1/2 cup unsalted butter, melted
- 1 tablespoon orange zest
- 1/4 cup fresh orange juice

Syrup:

- 1/2 cup granulated sugar
- 1/2 cup water
- 2 tablespoons honey
- 2 tablespoons orange juice

Topping:

- 1/4 cup sliced almonds
- 2 tablespoons honey, for drizzling

Directions:

1. Get started by setting your oven temperature to 350°F (175°C). Start by taking an 8-inch round cake pan and coating the interior with a light layer of grease. Then, line the bottom of the pan with a sheet of parchment paper.
2. Grab a medium-sized bowl and in it, whisk together the semolina flour, almond flour, baking powder, and salt.

3. Begin by using a hand mixer or stand mixer to beat eggs and sugar together in a large bowl until the mixture is light and airy. This should take about 2-3 minutes.
4. Slowly pour in the melted butter, orange zest, and orange juice, mixing until well combined.
5. Next, take the dry ingredients and gently fold them into the wet ingredients, mixing just until they are combined. Be careful not to overmix the batter.
6. With the batter fully prepared, transfer it to the cake pan that has been previously prepared. Grab a spatula and use it to gently spread the cake batter evenly across the surface of the prepared pan, smoothing the top.
7. Preheat your oven to the desired temperature. Once the oven is heated, transfer the prepared cake pan and place it inside. Let the cake bake for 40-45 minutes, periodically checking it by inserting a toothpick into the center.
8. While the cake is baking, make the syrup: In a small saucepan, combine the sugar, water, honey, and orange juice. First, heat the mixture over medium-high heat until it comes to a full boil. Once it's boiling, turn the heat down to low and let the mixture simmer for 5 minutes.
9. As soon as the cake comes out of the oven, immediately use a toothpick or skewer to poke a series of holes all over the top surface. Next, slowly pour the warm syrup over the hot cake, allowing it to gradually soak in.
10. Once the cake has cooled completely in the pan, carefully invert it onto a serving plate for presentation.
11. Sprinkle the sliced almonds over the top of the cake and drizzle with additional honey before serving.

Nutritional breakdown per serving:

Calories: 300 kcal, Protein: 6 grams, Carbohydrates: 40 grams, Fat: 15 grams, Saturated Fat: 6 grams, Cholesterol: 70 milligrams, Sodium: 100 milligrams, Fiber: 2 grams, and Sugar: 5 grams.

GRILLED MEDITERRANEAN FRUIT SALAD WITH HONEY-MINT SYRUP

Total Cooking Time: 25 minutes
Prep Time: 15 minutes
Servings: 6 (about 1 cup per serving)

Ingredients:

Fruit Salad:

- 1 medium pineapple, peeled, cored, and chopped into 1-inch slices
- 2 peaches, halved and pitted
- 2 nectarines, halved and pitted
- 1 mango, peeled, pitted, and diced into 1-inch cubes
- 1 red onion, sliced into 1/2-inch rings
- 2 tablespoons olive oil

Honey-Mint Syrup:

- 1/2 cup honey
- 1/4 cup water
- 2 tablespoons fresh lemon juice
- 1/4 cup fresh mint leaves, chopped

Instructions:

1. Get your grill or grill pan ready by preheating it to medium-high.
2. In a large bowl, combine the pineapple slices, peach halves, nectarine halves, mango cubes, and onion rings. Lightly pour olive oil over the ingredients and mix well to ensure even coverage.
3. Grill the fruit and onion for 2-3 minutes on each side, or until they are slightly charred and tender. Move the grilled mixture to a large serving bowl.
4. In a small saucepan, combine the honey, water, and lemon juice. Simmer the mixture over medium heat, stirring gently until the honey dissolves completely. This should take approximately 2-3 minutes. Once the mixture is off the heat, incorporate the chopped mint.
5. Drizzle the warm honey-mint syrup over the grilled fruit and onion in the serving bowl. Gently toss to coat.

6. Serve the Grilled Mediterranean Fruit Salad with Honey-Mint Syrup warm or at room temperature.

Nutritional breakdown per serving:

Calories: 220 kcal, Protein: 2 grams, Carbohydrates: 45 grams, Fat: 5 grams, Saturated Fat: 1 grams, Cholesterol: 0 milligrams, Sodium: 10 milligrams, Fiber: 4 grams, and Sugar: 5 grams.

MEDITERRANEAN OLIVE OIL AND SEA SALT CHOCOLATE TRUFFLES

Total Cooking Time: 1 hour 30 minutes
Prep Time: 30 minutes
Servings: 24 (1 truffle per serving)

Ingredients:

- 8 ounces of premium dark chocolate (70% cacao), chopped
- 1/2 cup heavy cream
- 2 tablespoons extra-virgin olive oil
- 1 teaspoon vanilla extract
- 1/4 teaspoon of sea salt, with additional salt for sprinkling
- Unsweetened cocoa powder, for dusting

Instructions:

1. In a medium heat-resistant bowl, whisk together the chopped dark chocolate and heavy cream. Nestle the bowl atop a pan of gently simmering water, ensuring no contact. Stir intermittently until the chocolate has fully melted and the mixture is smooth. This process typically takes 5-7 minutes.
2. Once the bowl is off the saucepan, incorporate the olive oil, vanilla extract, and 1/4 teaspoon of sea salt by stirring until they are fully blended.
3. Cover the bowl and place the chocolate mixture in the refrigerator for at least 1 hour, or until it is firm enough to scoop.
4. Place a sheet of parchment paper on a baking sheet.
5. With a small cookie scoop or spoon, form the chilled chocolate mixture into 1-inch balls and place them on the prepared baking sheet.
6. Place the truffles in the refrigerator for 30 more minutes, or until they are solid.
7. Roll the chilled truffles in unsweetened cocoa powder to coat them evenly.
8. Sprinkle the top of each truffle with a small pinch of sea salt.
9. Refrigerate the finished truffles until ready to serve, up to 1 week.

Nutritional breakdown per serving:

Calories: 90 kcal, Protein: 1 grams, Carbohydrates: 6 grams, Fat: 7 grams, Saturated Fat: 4 grams, Cholesterol: 10 milligrams, Sodium: 35 milligrams, Fiber: 1 grams, and Sugar: 5 grams.

BAKED MEDITERRANEAN ALMOND AND HONEY STUFFED APRICOTS

Total Cooking Time: 35 minutes
Prep Time: 15 minutes
Servings: 12 (1 stuffed apricot per serving)

Ingredients:

- 12 fresh apricots, halved and pitted
- 1/2 cup of raw unsalted almonds, chopped
- 2 tablespoons honey
- 1 teaspoon ground cinnamon
- 1/4 teaspoon ground cardamom
- Pinch of kosher salt

Instructions:

1. Get started by setting your oven temperature to 375°F (190°C). Line a baking sheet with parchment paper.
2. In a small bowl, mix together the chopped almonds, honey, cinnamon, cardamom, and salt until well combined.
3. Place the apricot halves, cut-side up, on the prepared baking sheet. Spoon a heaping teaspoon of the almond mixture into the center of each apricot half, gently pressing it into the cavity.
4. Bake the stuffed apricots for 20-25 minutes, or until the apricots are softened and the almond filling is lightly browned.
5. Remove the baked stuffed apricots from the oven and let them cool for 5 minutes before serving.

Nutritional breakdown per serving:

Calories: 50 kcal, Protein: 1 grams, Carbohydrates: 0 grams, Fat: 2 grams, Saturated Fat: 0 grams, Cholesterol: 0 milligrams, Sodium: 15 milligrams, Fiber: 1 grams, and Sugar: 5 grams.

MEDITERRANEAN LEMON AND OLIVE OIL POUND CAKE

Total Cooking Time: 1 hour 15 minutes
Prep Time: 20 minutes
Servings: 12 (1 slice per serving)

Ingredients:

- 2 cups all-purpose flour
- 1 teaspoon baking powder
- 1/4 teaspoon salt
- 3 large eggs
- 1 cup granulated sugar
- 1/2 cup extra-virgin olive oil
- 1/4 cup freshly squeezed lemon juice
- 2 tablespoons grated lemon zest
- 1 teaspoon vanilla extract

Instructions:

1. Get started by setting your oven temperature to 350°F (175°C). Butter or grease a 9x5-inch loaf pan.
2. Whisk together flour, baking powder, and salt in a medium bowl to create a harmonious blend of dry ingredients. Set this mixture aside for subsequent steps.
3. With an electric mixer on medium-high speed, beat the eggs and sugar together in a large bowl until the mixture is light and airy. Aim for 3-5 minutes of beating.
4. Gradually pour in the olive oil, lemon juice, lemon zest, and vanilla extract, beating well after each addition.
5. On low speed, gently incorporate the dry ingredients into the wet ingredients until they are just combined. Avoid overmixing.
6. Pour the batter into the prepared loaf pan and even out the top with a spatula.
7. Bake until a toothpick inserted into the center of the read comes out clean. This will takea bout 50-60 minutes.
8. Leave the cake to cool on the tray for 10 minutes, then slice and transfer to a rack to cool completely beforeserving.

Nutritional breakdown per serving:

Calories: 250 kcal, Protein: 4 grams, Carbohydrates: 32 grams, Fat: 12 grams, Saturated Fat: 3 grams, Cholesterol: 55 milligrams, Sodium: 125 milligrams, Fiber: 1 grams, and Sugar: 5 grams.

GRILLED MEDITERRANEAN FRUIT AND HALLOUMI SKEWERS WITH MINT YOGURT DIP

Total Cooking Time: 30 minutes
Prep Time: 20 minutes
Servings: 8 (2 skewers per serving)

Ingredients:

Skewers:

- 1 block (8 ounces) halloumi cheese, cut into 1-inch cubes
- 1 ripe peach, pitted and cut into 1-inch chunks
- 1 cup seedless grapes
- 1 cup cubed watermelon
- 1 tablespoon olive oil
- 1/2 teaspoon dried oregano
- Salt and pepper to taste

Mint Yogurt Dip:

- 1 cup plain Greek yogurt
- 2 tablespoons chopped fresh mint leaves
- 1 tablespoon lemon juice
- 1 garlic clove, minced
- Pinch of salt

Instructions:

1. Get your grill or grill pan ready by preheating it to medium-high.
2. Assemble the olive oil, oregano, salt, pepper, halloumi, peaches, grapes, and watermelon in a medium bowl and mix thoroughly.
3. Thread the marinated ingredients onto skewers, alternating the different fruits and halloumi.
4. Grill the skewers for 2-3 minutes per side, or until the halloumi is lightly charred and the fruits are slightly softened.
5. Create a harmonious blend of flavors by whisking together strained yogurt, finely chopped mint, tangy lemon juice, minced garlic, and a pinch of salt in a small bowl.

6. Serve the grilled skewers immediately, with the mint yogurt dip on the side for dipping.

Nutritional breakdown per serving:

Calories: 180 kcal, Protein: 10 grams, Carbohydrates: 15 grams, Fat: 10 grams, Saturated Fat: 6 grams, Cholesterol: 30 milligrams, Sodium: 320 milligrams, Fiber: 1 grams, and Sugar: 5 grams.

BAKED MEDITERRANEAN PISTACHIO AND DATE BAKLAVA ROLLS

Total Cooking Time: 1 hour 15 minutes
Prep Time: 30 minutes
Servings: 16 (1 roll per serving)

Ingredients:

- 1 cup shelled pistachios, finely chopped
- 1 cup chopped pitted dates
- 1/4 cup granulated sugar
- 1 teaspoon ground cinnamon
- 1/4 teaspoon ground cloves
- 1/4 teaspoon ground cardamom
- 16 sheets phyllo dough, thawed if frozen
- 1/2 cup unsalted butter, melted
- 1/2 cup honey

Syrup:

- 1/2 cup water
- 1/2 cup granulated sugar
- 2 tablespoons lemon juice

Instructions:

1. Get started by setting your oven temperature to 350°F (175°C). Line a baking sheet with parchment paper.
2. Assemble the chopped pistachios, chopped dates, ¼ cup of sugar, cinnamon, cloves, and cardamom in a medium bowl and mix until well blended.
3. Lay one phyllo sheet on a clean work surface and brushlightly with melted butter. Place another phylloon top and brush with a little more butter.
4. Spread about 2-3 tablespoons of the pistachio-date filling in a line along the long edge of the phyllo sheets, leaving a 1-inch border on the sides.
5. Carefully roll up the phyllo sheets tightly around the filling, starting from the filled edge and rolling towards the opposite side. Place the rolled baklava seam-side down on the prepared baking sheet.
6. Repeat steps 3 - 5 with the remaining phyllo and filling to make a total of 16 rolls.

7. Bake the baklava rolls for 30-35 minutes or until golden brown.
8. Simultaneously with the baking of the baklava, prepare the syrup. Put the water, 1/2 cup sugar and lemon juice in a small saucepan. Bring to the boil, reduce the heat and simmer for 5 minutes, stirring occasionally.
9. Remove the baked baklava rolls from the oven and immediately drizzle the warm honey over the top.
10. Drizzle the prepared syrup over the hot baklava rolls and let them cool for at least 30 minutes before serving.

Nutritional breakdown per serving:

Calories: 230 kcal, Protein: 3 grams, Carbohydrates: 31 grams, Fat: 11 grams, Saturated Fat: 4 grams, Cholesterol: 15 milligrams, Sodium: 55 milligrams, Fiber: 2 grams, and Sugar: 5 grams.

MEDITERRANEAN ALMOND AND ORANGE BLOSSOM WATER MERINGUES

Total Cooking Time: 3 hours (including cooling time)
Prep Time: 30 minutes
Servings: 16 (1 meringue per serving)

Ingredients:

- 3 large egg whites, at room temperature
- 3/4 cup (150g) granulated sugar
- 1/4 cup (25g) sliced almonds, toasted
- 1 teaspoon orange blossom water
- 1/4 teaspoon cream of tartar

Garnish:

- 2 tablespoons sliced almonds, toasted
- Zest of 1 orange

Instructions:

1. Get started by setting your oven temperature to 200°F (95°C). Line a baking sheet with parchment paper.
2. To start, whisk the egg whites in a clean, dry bowl until they become soft and fluffy.
3. As you whisk, gradually add the cream of tartar until the mixture reaches soft peaks in approximately 2-3 minutes.
4. To achieve stiff, glossy peaks, gradually introduce the granulated sugar, one tablespoon at a time, while whisking vigorously. This process should take approximately 5-7 minutes.
5. Fold in the 1/4 cup of toasted sliced almonds and the orange blossom water until just combined.
6. Carefully scoop the meringue mixture onto the prepared baking sheet, forming 16 equal mounds that are spaced approximately 2 inches apart.
7. Bake the meringues for 2 hours, or until they are dry and crisp on the outside. Turn off the oven and leave the meringues inside with the door closed for an additional 1 hour to continue drying.
8. Let the meringues cool undisturbed on the baking sheet for about 30 minutes before removing them.

9. Garnish the cooled meringues with the remaining 2 tablespoons of toasted sliced almonds and the orange zest.

Nutritional breakdown per serving:

Calories: 80 kcal, Protein: 1 grams, Carbohydrates: 14 grams, Fat: 2 grams, Saturated Fat: 0 grams, Cholesterol: 0 milligrams, Sodium: 10 milligrams, Fiber: 1 grams, and Sugar: 5 grams.

GRILLED MEDITERRANEAN FIGS WITH HONEY AND MASCARPONE

Total Cooking Time: 20 minutes
Prep Time: 10 minutes
Servings: 8 (2 figs per serving)

Ingredients:

- 16 fresh figs, halved lengthwise
- 2 tablespoons olive oil
- 1/4 cup honey
- 1/2 cup mascarpone cheese
- 2 tablespoons chopped pistachios
- 1 tablespoon chopped fresh mint

Instructions:

1. Get your grill or grill pan ready by preheating it to medium-high.
2. Brush the cut sides of the figs with the olive oil.
3. Place the figs, cut-side down, on the preheated grill and cook for 2-3 minutes, or until grill marks appear.
4. Flip the figs and cook for an additional 1-2 minutes, or until they are slightly softened.
5. Transfer the grilled figs to a serving platter.
6. Drizzle the warm figs with the honey.
7. Top each fig half with a dollop of mascarpone cheese.
8. Sprinkle the chopped pistachios and fresh mint over the top.
9. Serve the grilled Mediterranean figs immediately, while still warm.

Nutritional breakdown per serving:

Calories: 160 kcal, Protein: 3 grams, Carbohydrates: 23 grams, Fat: 7 grams, Saturated Fat: 4 grams, Cholesterol: 20 milligrams, Sodium: 15 milligrams, Fiber: 3 grams, and Sugar: 5 grams.

BAKED MEDITERRANEAN OLIVE OIL AND SEA SALT SHORTBREAD COOKIES

Total Cooking Time: 45 minutes
Prep Time: 20 minutes
Servings: 24 (1 cookie per serving)

Ingredients:

- 2 cups (250g) all-purpose flour
- 1/2 cup (100g) granulated sugar
- 1/2 teaspoon sea salt, extra for sprinkling
- 3/4 cup (180ml) good-quality extra-virgin olive oil
- 1 teaspoon vanilla extract

Instructions:

1. Get started by setting your oven temperature to 325°F (160°C). Cover a baking sheet with parchment paper.
2. To a spacious mixing bowl, add the flour, granulated sugar, and a half teaspoon of sea salt. Whisk vigorously until all ingredients are thoroughly blended.
3. Combine the olive oil and vanilla extract with the dry ingredients and mix until a dough comes together. The dough will have a slightly crumbly texture, but it should still hold together when pressed.
4. Transfer the dough to a floured board and give it a brief kneading.
5. Gently gather the dough onto a floured countertop and knead a few times to form a cohesive mass.
6. Employ a 2-inch round cookie cutter to shape the dough into cookies. If necessary, re-roll the trimmings.
7. Distribute the cookies evenly on the baking sheet, maintaining a distance of about 1 inch.
8. Bake the cookies for 20-22 minutes, or until they are lightly golden around the edges.
9. After baking, adorn the cookies with a delicate sprinkling of sea salt.
10. Cool cookies on baking sheet for 5 minutes, then transfer to wire rack.

Nutritional breakdown per serving:

Calories: 120 kcal, Protein: 1 grams, Carbohydrates: 13 grams, Fat: 7 grams, Saturated Fat: 1 grams, Cholesterol: 0 milligrams, Sodium: 65 milligrams, Fiber: 1 grams, and Sugar: 5 grams.

MEDITERRANEAN LEMON AND LAVENDER POSSET

Total Cooking Time: 30 minutes (plus 4 hours chilling time)
Prep Time: 15 minutes
Servings: 6 (1/2 cup per serving)

Ingredients:

- 2 cups (480ml) heavy cream
- 3/4 cup (150g) granulated sugar
- 1/4 cup (60ml) fresh lemon juice (from approximately 2 lemons)
- 1 tablespoon dried lavender, extra for garnish
- 1 teaspoon lemon zest, extra for garnish

Instructions:

1. Assemble the heavy cream and granulated sugar in a medium saucepan. Position the pan over medium heat and allow the mixture to simmer, stirring periodically, until the sugar has completely dissolved. This process should take approximately 5 minutes.
2. Withdraw the pan from the heat and incorporate the lemon juice, 1 tablespoon of dried lavender buds, and the 1 teaspoon of grated lemon zest. Whisk the mixture until it is fully blended.
3. Carefully pour the posset into six 1/2 cup (120ml) ramekins or small glasses.
4. Seal the ramekins with plastic wrap and place them in the refrigerator for a minimum of 4 hours, or until the posset has set and is thoroughly chilled.
5. When you are prepared to serve the posset, take it out of the refrigerator. Garnish each portion with a sprinkle of additional dried lavender buds and lemon zest.

Nutritional breakdown per serving:

Calories: 330 kcal, Protein: 2 grams, Carbohydrates: 30 grams, Fat: 24 grams, Saturated Fat: 15 grams, Cholesterol: 85 milligrams, Sodium: 20 milligrams, Fiber: 1 grams, and Sugar: 5 grams.

GRILLED MEDITERRANEAN FRUIT AND HALLOUMI SKEWERS WITH POMEGRANATE MOLASSES GLAZE

Total Cooking Time: 25 minutes
Prep Time: 20 minutes
Servings: 6 (2 skewers per serving)

Ingredients:

- 12 ounces (340g) halloumi cheese, cut into 1-inch cubes
- 1 cup (150g) fresh pineapple chunks
- 1 cup (150g) fresh cantaloupe chunks
- 1 cup (150g) fresh watermelon chunks
- 1/4 cup (60ml) pomegranate molasses
- 2 tablespoons olive oil
- 1 tablespoon fresh lemon juice
- 1 teaspoon dried oregano
- 1/4 teaspoon ground cinnamon
- Salt and pepper to taste
- Wooden skewers (soaked 30 minutes)

Instructions:

1. Get your grill or grill pan ready by preheating it to medium-high.
2. Assemble the pomegranate molasses, olive oil, lemon juice, oregano, and cinnamon in a small bowl. Season with salt and pepper to taste. Whisk the mixture until it is fully blended.
3. Thread the halloumi, pineapple, cantaloupe, and watermelon onto the soaked wooden skewers, alternating the ingredients.
4. Grill the skewers for 2-3 minutes per side, basting them with the pomegranate molasses glaze during the last minute of cooking.
5. Move the grilled skewers to a serving platter and generously drizzle any leftover glaze over the top.
6. Serve the Grilled Mediterranean Fruit and Halloumi Skewers immediately, while still warm.

Nutritional breakdown per serving:

Calories: 280 kcal, Protein: 14 grams, Carbohydrates: 28 grams, Fat: 15 grams, Saturated Fat: 8 grams, Cholesterol: 40 milligrams, Sodium: 620 milligrams, Fiber: 1 grams, and Sugar: 5 grams.

BAKED MEDITERRANEAN ALMOND AND HONEY BAKLAVA BITES

Total Cooking Time: 60 minutes
Prep Time: 30 minutes
Servings: 20 (1 bite per serving)

Ingredients:

- 1 cup (140g) chopped raw almonds
- 1/2 cup (100g) granulated sugar
- 1 teaspoon ground cinnamon
- 1/4 teaspoon ground cloves
- 1/8 teaspoon ground nutmeg
- 8 sheets phyllo dough, thawed if frozen
- 1/2 cup (120ml) unsalted butter, melted
- 1/2 cup (120ml) honey
- 2 tablespoons water

Instructions:

1. Get started by setting your oven temperature to 350°F (175°C). Grease a 24-cup mini muffin tin.
2. Process the almonds in a food processor until they are finely chopped, but not reduced to a powder. Transfer the chopped almonds to a small bowl and incorporate the granulated sugar, cinnamon, cloves, and nutmeg. Reserve the mixture.
3. Unroll phyllo, cover with damp towel. Working with one sheet at a time, brush the phyllo with melted butter and cut into 4 even strips. Place a strip of phyllo into each mini muffin cup, gently pressing it into the sides to form a cup shape.
4. Spoon about 1 tablespoon of the almond mixture into each phyllo cup.
5. In a small saucepan, combine the honey and water. Position the pan over medium heat and allow the mixture to simmer, stirring periodically, until it has thickened slightly. This process should take approximately 2-3 minutes.
6. Drizzle a teaspoon of the honey mixture over the almond filling in each phyllo cup.
7. Bake baklava bites until golden brown and crisp (18-20 minutes).
8. Withdraw the baklava bites from the oven and allow them to rest in the muffin tin for 5 minutes. Subsequently, relocate them to a wire rack for complete cooling.

Nutritional breakdown per serving:

Calories: 90 kcal, Protein: 1 grams, Carbohydrates: 10 grams, Fat: 5 grams, Saturated Fat: 2 grams, Cholesterol: 5 milligrams, Sodium: 5 milligrams, Fiber: 1 grams, and Sugar: 5 grams.

MEDITERRANEAN LEMON AND OLIVE OIL RICOTTA CAKE

Total Cooking Time: 1 hour 10 minutes
Prep Time: 20 minutes
Servings: 12 (1 slice per serving)

Ingredients:

- 1 1/2 cups (190g) all-purpose flour
- 1 teaspoon baking powder
- 1/4 teaspoon salt
- 3 large eggs
- 1 cup (200g) granulated sugar
- 1 cup (240g) whole-milk ricotta cheese
- 1/2 cup (120ml) extra-virgin olive oil
- 2 tablespoons lemon juice
- 1 tablespoon grated lemon zest
- 1 teaspoon vanilla extract
- Powdered sugar for dusting

Instructions:

1. Get started by setting your oven temperature to 350°F (175°C). Line a greased 9-inch round baking pan with parchment paper.
2. In a medium bowl, whisk together the flour, baking powder, and salt to create a harmonious blend of dry ingredients. Set this mixture aside for later use.
3. In a large bowl, vigorously beat the eggs and granulated sugar using an electric mixer set on high speed until the mixture becomes light and airy. This process should take approximately 3-4 minutes.
4. Reduce the speed of the electric mixer and gently fold in the ricotta cheese, olive oil, lemon juice, lemon zest, and vanilla extract. Incorporate the ingredients together until they are completely unified.
5. Having introduced the dry ingredients to the wet ingredients, mix them gently until they are fully integrated. Avoid overmixing.
6. Spread the batter across the prepared baking pan like a blanket, smoothing out any wrinkles or lumps.
7. Bake the cake until it is as light and fluffy as a cloud and a toothpick inserted into its center comes out clean, like a feather floating through the air.

8. Let the cake rest in the pan for 10 minutes. Subsequently, relocate it to a wire rack for complete cooling.
9. Adorn the top of the cake with powdered sugar before serving.

Nutritional breakdown per serving:

Calories: 260 kcal, Protein: 6 grams, Carbohydrates: 28 grams, Fat: 14 grams, Saturated Fat: 3.5 grams, Cholesterol: 65 milligrams, Sodium: 135 milligrams, Fiber: 1 grams, and Sugar: 5 grams.

GRILLED MEDITERRANEAN FRUIT AND MASCARPONE STUFFED FIGS

Total Cooking Time: 30 minutes
Prep Time: 15 minutes
Servings: 12 (1 stuffed fig per serving)

Ingredients:

- 12 fresh figs, halved lengthwise
- 1/2 cup (120g) mascarpone cheese
- 2 tablespoons honey
- 1 tablespoon lemon zest
- 1/4 teaspoon ground cinnamon
- 1/4 cup (60ml) balsamic glaze
- 1/4 cup (35g) chopped toasted pistachios

Instructions:

1. Get your grill or grill pan ready by preheating it to medium-high.
2. Add the mascarpone cheese, honey, lemon zest, and cinnamon to a small bowl. Whisk the ingredients until thoroughly mixed.
3. Carefully spoon or pipe about 1-2 tablespoons of the mascarpone mixture into the center of each fig half.
4. Grill the stuffed figs, cut-side down, for 2-3 minutes, or until grill marks appear.
5. Carefully flip the figs and grill for an additional 1-2 minutes, or until the figs are slightly softened.
6. Transfer the grilled, stuffed figs to a serving platter.
7. Drizzle the balsamic glaze over the top of the figs.
8. Sprinkle the chopped pistachios over the figs, and serve immediately.

Nutritional breakdown per serving:

Calories: 100 kcal, Protein: 2 grams, Carbohydrates: 13 grams, Fat: 5 grams, Saturated Fat: 3 grams, Cholesterol: 10 milligrams, Sodium: 15 milligrams, Fiber: 2 grams, and Sugar: 5 grams.

BAKED MEDITERRANEAN PISTACHIO AND ORANGE BLOSSOM SEMOLINA CAKE

Total Cooking Time: 1 hour 15 minutes
Prep Time: 30 minutes
Servings: 12 (1 slice per serving)

Ingredients:

- 1 cup (150g) semolina flour
- 3/4 cup (150g) granulated sugar
- 1/2 cup (120ml) orange juice
- 1/2 cup (120ml) vegetable oil
- 1/4 cup (60ml) orange blossom water
- 2 large eggs
- 1 teaspoon baking powder
- 1/4 teaspoon salt
- 1 cup (140g) chopped pistachios, plus more for garnish
- Powdered sugar for dusting

Instructions:

1. Get started by setting your oven temperature to 350°F (175°C). Coat a 9-inch round baking pan with grease and flour.
2. Add the semolina flour, granulated sugar, baking powder, and salt to a large bowl. Whisk the ingredients together until they are fully blended.
3. Add the orange juice, vegetable oil, orange blossom water, and eggs to a separate bowl. Mix the ingredients together until they are well blended.
4. Combine the wet and dry ingredients. Stir the mixture together carefully until it is just combined, being cautious not to overmix.
5. Fold in the chopped pistachios.
6. Spread the batter evenly over the top of the prepared baking pan.
7. Insert a toothpick into the center of the cake. Bake until the toothpick comes out clean, indicating the cake is fully cooked. This usually takes 45 to 55 minutes.
8. Once the cake has cooled for 10 minutes, carefully lift it from the pan and place it on a wire rack to finish cooling.
9. Once the cake is cool, sprinkle the top with powdered sugar and chopped pistachios.

Nutritional breakdown per serving:

Calories: 320 kcal, Protein: 6 grams, Carbohydrates: 37 grams, Fat: 17 grams, Saturated Fat: 2 grams, Cholesterol: 45 milligrams, Sodium: 130 milligrams, Fiber: 2 grams, and Sugar: 5 grams.

CONCLUSION

As we conclude our journey through the "150 Recipes for Mediterranean Diet Meal Prep Cookbook," it's clear that adopting this way of eating is about more than just preparing meals—it's about embracing a vibrant lifestyle that nurtures both body and soul. The Mediterranean diet is a celebration of flavor, health, and community, encouraging us to connect with our food and those we share it with.

Throughout this cookbook, you have explored a diverse array of recipes, each designed to make meal preparation not only efficient but also enjoyable. From savory dishes that highlight the rich spices and fresh produce of the Mediterranean region to wholesome snacks that satisfy cravings without compromising health, every recipe is a step toward transforming your culinary habits. The emphasis on seasonal ingredients and simple preparations allows for a sustainable approach to cooking that anyone can incorporate into their busy lives.

The advantages of the Mediterranean diet reach well beyond just meal preparation. By focusing on whole foods, nutritious fats, and plant-based ingredients, you are making important progress in boosting your heart health, lowering the chances of chronic illnesses, and improving your overall wellness. This dietary approach promotes not just physical health but also mental wellness, encouraging mindfulness, balance, and enjoyment in every meal.

As you continue to enjoy the recipes within these pages, remember that meal prep is not just about convenience; it's an opportunity to savor the process of cooking and to take pride in what you nourish your body with. Engage with your ingredients, experiment with flavors, and don't hesitate to make each recipe your own. The Mediterranean lifestyle is about sharing meals with loved ones, creating memories around the table, and appreciating the simple joys of life.

We hope this cookbook inspires you to embrace the Mediterranean way of eating and to make it a lasting part of your routine. With 150 tasty and wholesome recipes available to you, you have everything you need to prepare fulfilling meals that will help maintain your energy and health. So, gather your loved ones, explore the culinary treasures of the Mediterranean, and enjoy the journey to a healthier, happier you!

Made in the USA
Middletown, DE
19 July 2025